Medieval and Renaissance Series
Number 5

MEDIEVAL

AND

RENAISSANCE STUDIES

Proceedings of the Southeastern Institute
of Medieval and Renaissance Studies
Summer, 1969

Edited by O. B. Hardison, Jr.

The University of North Carolina Press · Chapel Hill

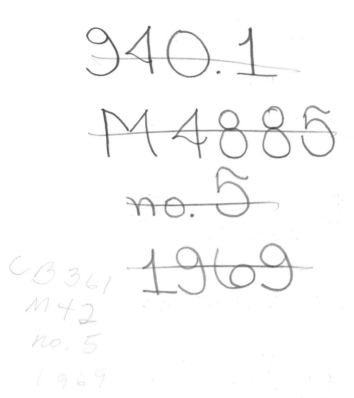

Manufactured in the United States of America
Printed by the Seeman Printery, Durham, N.C.
ISBN 0-8078-1172-6
Library of Congress Catalog Card Number 66-25361

To
JOHN LEON LIEVSAY
without whom the Institute
would never have become a reality.

Foreword

This volume, the fifth in its series, constitutes a valediction to the Southeastern Institute of Medieval and Renaissance Studies. The Institute was established in 1965 as a cooperative venture between Duke University and The University of North Carolina at Chapel Hill.

Supported by the Ford Foundation and, during its last two years, by a supplementary grant from the National Endowment of the Humanities, the Institute was initiated as an experiment in continuing education in the humanities. Its founders believed that teaching and research are inseparable and that one key to stimulating performance in the classroom is the teacher's sense of engagement with the vital intellectual issues raised by the subject treated. Too often scholars are given specialized training during the Ph.D. program, only to have this training wasted when they leave graduate school for small colleges where research facilities are limited, where most of their teaching is in courses for which specialized skills are superfluous, and where there is little opportunity to contact individuals with similar interests. The result can be a growing sense of isolation which leads to a loss of the creative involvement and commitment which graduate training attempts to instill. The danger is that the passionately involved younger scholar may become a middle-aged drudge. When this happens, of course, the classroom atmosphere changes. An adventure becomes a routine. The exciting feeling of being on the cutting edge of intellectual and cultural activity is lost. The student, of course, is the prime loser if this happens. Excitement (and *in*citement to further, independent development) gives way to boredom. The results are all too familiar.

Continuing education in the humanities is not the solution to all of the problems which currently beset the humanities, but it certainly must be a major component in any future approach to these problems. Ironically, continuing education is already institutionalized for most high school teachers and for college teachers in the sciences, in law, in medicine, and even in business schools. The humanities, it seems, are expected to flourish without cultivation. They are the first subjects to suffer from a budgetary crisis, the first to be cut back in any rearrangement of institutional or national priorities. Apparently, in the humanities, class size can always be enlarged, teacher-student ratios can always be increased, faculty positions can always be eliminated, and research opportunities—which are basically opportunities for the teacher to renew his sense of involvement and upgrade his skills—can always be reduced. The question is how long this can continue without the humanities curriculum becoming an empty ritual in which students register for meaningless courses and eventually receive meaningless degrees, simply because a degree—any degree—is a ticket to the job market.

The Southeastern Institute was an attempt to counter this trend. All of those associated with it are grateful to the Ford Foundation and to the National Endowment for supporting its commitment and for sharing, in some measure, its belief in the importance of continuing education in the humanities. In practice, the Institute proved successful beyond the hopes of its founders. During its five sessions, thirty-seven seminars were offered by such distinguished scholars as Sir Steven Runciman, F. L. Ganshof, Lynn White, Richard Sylvester, Otis Green, Paul Oskar Kristeller, John Lievsay, Aldo Scaglione, and others. Over two hundred Fellows from every state in the Southeastern region and from every type of institution—from seminary to four-year liberal arts, to university—enrolled. The record of the seminars, the participants, and the public lectures which were a regular feature of the Institute is preserved in the five volumes of proceedings, of which this is the last. It may be added that the final summer of the Institute indicated that the need for and interest in its program had not diminished over the years, since approximately three applications were received for every seminar position.

Special thanks for assistance during the 1969 session are due to several individuals. Professor Dale Randall of Duke University, the Co-Chairman for the session, shared the burdens of administration equally with the Chairman, and his work was invaluable in assuring the success of the program. The Joint Central Committee of the Duke-Chapel Hill Cooperative Program in the Humanities, under the chairmanship of Professor James Godfrey of Chapel Hill, provided its usual measure of support and assistance. The Institute Committee, consisting of Professors Philip Fehl, Aldo Scaglione, and John Headley of Chapel Hill, and Arthur Ferguson and Hans Hillerbrand of Duke, provided a large measure of guidance in addition to assisting in the many tasks that were a necessary prelude to the session proper. Finally, all participants wish to express their gratitude to the two universities for their encouragement of what we hope is in some measure a pattern for future support of humanistic education.

O. B. Hardison, Jr.
Folger Shakespeare Library
May 14, 1970

Contents

[xi]

MEDIEVAL
AND
RENAISSANCE STUDIES

I

Medieval Borrowings from Further Asia

Lynn White, jr.

University of California, Los Angeles

Ex oriente lux: that light comes from the East was axiomatic in the European West during the millennium before Columbus and Vasco da Gama opened the era of occidental world conquest. Adherents of the Latin Church were revolted by what they regarded as the religious errors of Byzantines, Muslims and the more distant idolaters; nevertheless they were far more receptive to Eastern innovations than their descendents since 1500 have been.

This medieval attitude must be understood in its geographic context. Japan in the same period was equally open to external influences; yet its axiom might have been *ex occidente lux,* since innovations came from such "Western" lands as Korea, China, India, even Iran. Eurasia was a garland of flourishing and individually creative cultures, each of which influenced all the others normally, though not always, in proportion to adjacency. The fact that medieval Europe and Japan absorbed so much from East and West respectively, does not imply lack of creativity in the Japanese or Europeans of that period: it is largely a function of their locations.

The medieval West, in fact, produced a few novelties which penetrated not only the Greek- and Arabic-speaking regions but even further eastward. Before the First Crusade both Muslims and Byzantines were already beginning to absorb elements of the new technique of mounted shock combat which the Westerners had been developing since the eighth

[3]

century.[1] While the crossbow may have reached the Roman world from China, a new and more effective form of it emerged in the eleventh-century West: in Byzantium, Moorish Spain and even South India it was regarded as distinctively Frankish.[2] Under the Yuan dynasty, the Italian twelfth-century art of distilling alcohol reached China.[3] About A.D. 1480 the Persian poet Jāmī, although doubtless unaware that eyeglasses had been invented in Tuscany two hundred years earlier, nevertheless knew that they were Frankish.[4] As oriental studies increase in volume and depth, understanding of Western medieval influences moving eastward will doubtless be augmented.

The problem of cultural osmosis from Byzantium and Islam to the West is complicated by the fact that these three sister civilizations were all constructed primarily of the same Hellenistic, Roman and Semitic elements in varying proportions. The medieval Greek world displays complete continuity with the Roman East. Islam, moreover, was not a meteoric invasion from outer space: it was produced by a Semitic community deeply influenced by Judaism and Hellenism and, in Muhammad's day, by the Christian Ethiopic empire. When the Islamic armies swept over Syria, Egypt, North Africa and Spain, they brought new vigor to populations which for centuries continued to be in large part Christian. The leading post-patristic theologian of the Eastern Church, St. John of Damascus, lived and died a subject of the Caliph. From the eleventh century onward a great wave of translation of scientific and philosophical materials from Arabic into Latin led to the paradox that the influence of such geniuses as al-Rāzī, ibn al-Haitam and ibn Rushd has been greater in the West than in Islam itself. When in 1389 the great Paduan professor of medicine and astronomy Giovanni de'Dondi died, 23 of the 110 books in his personal library were Latin translations from the Arabic,[5] and this was quite typical for such a person in Europe at that time.

It is an anachronism to project into the Western Middle Ages the contempt for the Near East that has characterized the Occident in more recent centuries. Despite intense antag-

[4]

onisms, medieval modes of life, kinds of piety and intellectual interests were closely akin from Iran to Ireland. For a century the court of the Norman kings at Palermo kept written records with equal facility in Latin, Greek and Arabic, and used French as a casual vernacular. The modern dichotomy of East and West has little meaning to an historian of the Middle Ages, and the question of cultural borrowings among Franks, Muslims and Byzantines is reduced almost to the level of neighborly exchange. We shall therefore focus out attention on medieval Europe's debt to southern, central and eastern Asia.

* * * * *

The effort to estimate the extent of this debt is plagued by the hypothesis that parallel invention is frequent, arising out of common human needs. Parallel invention is at times demonstrable, as in the case of the independent Babylonian and Mayan mathematical zeros. Nevertheless, as scholarship becomes more international, networks of connections grow more evident. The hen was domesticated on the southern slopes of the Himilayas,[6] and by the later Middle Ages chickens were known from Hawaii to Iceland. If this versatile Indian fowl could travel so widely, there is no a priori reason for doubting that many other elements of Indic culture followed the same routes. Yet, for example, does the three-faced representation of the Holy Trinity, which is found in Europe from the twelfth century until 1628, when it was banned by Pope Urban VIII as "monstrous," reflect the Indian *Trimurti?* This would seem to be an authentic instance of parellelism: the *Trimurti* image has three full faces; the Western analogy often has three faces represented by consolidating three noses and mouths with four eyes, and this form is clearly derived from Celtic images of a three-faced god.[7] If India and Europe are connected in this instance, the link must be found in migrations and diffusions long antedating the Middle Ages. In judging questions of diffusion versus parallel development, no general considerations can be applied. Each case must be decided on the basis of the specific evidence available.

[5]

Since complex parallelisms have emerged in cultures distant from each other, anthropologists sometimes use the hypothesis that "stimulus diffusion" may convey a basic idea (e.g., the windmill, or printing) without transmitting its implementation. If the inventor of the European, horizontal-axle windmill, who lived along the shores of the North Sea in the 1180's heard of the vertical-axle windmills which, since the tenth century, had been known in Afghanistan, it is curious that we have no firm evidence that windmills of any sort were ever used in medieval Islam west of the Helmand valley. Although German crusaders took the Western windmill to Syria in 1192,[8] thirteen years later in Northern Mesopotamia the leading Arabic technological writer of his age, al-Jazarī, explicitly denies that it is feasible to operate mills by wind-power.[9] Similarly, while it seems incredible that there is no direct connection between Korean printing with cast moveable type in the 1390's and Gutenberg's activities in Mainz fifty years later, such appears to be the case.[10] The European use of the press, which was not employed in East Asia for printing before the nineteenth century, is a symptom of the independence of the European invention. The hypothesis of "stimulus diffusion" is attractive, but it is also intellectually dangerous because it offers the illusion of understanding relations between discrete events that we cannot connect by means of concrete facts.

Nevertheless, specific evidence available to us indicates continuity of contacts between the major communities of Eurasia. Small radio-active inclusions in some of the garnets so popular in Merovingian jewelry probably prove that they came from Ceylon.[11] About A.D. 973 a Muslim visitor to Mainz expressed amazement at the variety of Indonesian spices available in its market.[12] Doubtless such commodities passed through the hands of many middlemen; but such is the normal pattern of cultural diffusion as well. And, despite the great difficulties and perils of travel, adventurous men continued to journey widely, although lamentably few have left to us accounts of their wanderings. In 883 King Alfred sent a delegation of Anglo-

Saxons with alms for the shrine of St. Thomas near Madras. One survived to return with jewels and become a bishop.[13] Documents from the Old Synagogue of Cairo picture Jewish merchants of the twelfth and thirteenth centuries travelling from Spain and Sicily to Egypt in Pisan and Genoese vessels and then going on to India quite habitually.[14] Matthew Paris, the gossipy chronicler of St. Albans in the middle of the thirteenth century, casually relates his conversations with two groups of Armenians—one of clerics, the other of merchants— who were travelling in England, and this at a time when Armenians were also ranging deep into Asia.[15] Everyone has heard of Marco Polo; few know that in the 1330's Italian Franciscan friars had two convents in Zayton on the coast of Fukien.[16] Many Genoese and Venetians penetrated India;[17] indeed, in 1444–48 a Sicilian named Pietro Rambulo led an embassy of the Negus of Ethiopia to India and Ceylon.[18] In 1497, the year before Vasco da Gama reached Calicut, a Genoese merchant who had got into legal difficulties in Sumatra was defended in the local courts by a Muslim lawyer who spoke some Italian.[19]

Historians are traditionally trained with such intensity to respect written texts that they often forgot that only a small part of human experience has ever been recorded. The Chinese belt-clasp from a Merovingian grave,[20] the small North-Indian image of Buddha found in a Swedish Viking settlement,[21] the remarkably authentic elephant howdah carved on the fifteenth-century choir stalls of Ripon Cathedral:[22] all of these speak, for our purposes, as loudly as any words. Together with the scattered available texts, they tell of communication, however slender, between Europe and the more distant parts of Asia throughout the Middle Ages.

Nevertheless by no means all the claims of European indebtedness to the Orient can be substantiated. Histories of ships, for example, have often asserted that the first example of the fore-and-aft rig, which permits sharp tacking into the wind, was the lateen sail, and that this was brought by the Muslims from the Indian Ocean to the Mediterranean. Recently, however, fore-and-aft rigs of several sorts, including lateen, have been found on small boats from the Aegean to Ostia under the early Roman Empire. Perhaps because the design of keels lagged behind that of rigging, lateens were not used on merchant ships until the sixth century, when they are found at Marseilles.[23] Since the word *lateen* is derived from the rare Latin *latinus* meaning "easy, handy,"[24] the lateen sail may be a Western invention which was diffused eastward to the dhows of the Indian Ocean. In the subsequent discussion, I shall omit negative results of this sort.

* * * * *

In the present state of scholarship, what borrowings by medieval Europe can be traced, either with certainty or with reasonable probability, to the further Orient? When did each arrive in the West, and by what route? What, if any, influence did each exert in shaping occidental life?

The following swift inventory, with minor exceptions, will be arranged not topically, but roughly by centuries in an effort to identify temporal clusters of diffusions westward. Some items are clearly diffusions; in other cases, the possibility of parallel invention in East and West cannot yet be eliminated entirely. However, if a doubtful item appears at a time and place where other evidences of European contacts with eastern, southern or central Asia are found, the probability of diffusion is increased. Quite arbitrarily we shall begin with the sixth century of our era.

Since the later years of the Roman Republic, one of the most precious commodities imported by the West had been silk; but Chinese export prohibitions and the chronic warfare between Iran and Rome (later, Byzantium) made the supply uncertain. About 554 the Emperor Justinian managed to secure silk worms smuggled to Byzantium by Christian monks, probably from Khotan where, a century earlier, sericulture had been established by means of cocoons secreted in the elaborate coiffure of a Chinese princess who came to marry the prince of that city.[25] Evidently the white mulberry tree, the essential food of the silk worm, was already known in the Aegean area. With amazing rapidity the manufacture of silk became a major industry in several centers of the Greek Empire, but always under close governmental control to prevent its precious secrets from spreading farther westward.[26] Nevertheless by the early twelfth century some silk worms were being raised in Norman Sicily, and when in 1147 Roger II of Sicily plundered Corfu, Corinth and Thebes, he took back to Palermo a large group of Greek prisoners skilled in silk production and manufacture.[27] Cultivation of the silk worm had already reached Brescia by the tenth century,[28] and from the later thirteenth century onward silk was fundamental to the prosperity of Tuscany and the Po Valley, spreading also to the Rhone in the fourteenth century. The arrival of the silk worm in Constantinople in the middle of the sixth century therefore inaugurated a new epoch in European textiles.

Economically less significant, but even more surprising, is the information given us by Paul the Deacon that about 600, to the astonishment of the people of Italy, the Lombards imported to that peninsula the domesticated Indian buffalo, which serves today as the source of mozarella. The use of buffaloes in the Near East at that time is uncertain. Since their introduction is associated by Paul with that of wild horses, and since by Aristotle's time buffaloes had reached Afghanistan, they may have been transmitted to Italy by routes north of the Caspian.[29]

The seventh century seems barren of Eastern borrowings, but in the eighth century a remarkable group of inventions related to the use of horses reached Europe from Asia.

In the second century before Christ the big-toe stirrup came into use in India, and eventually it spread wherever Indic culture made contact with barefoot aristocracies: from Timor in the east to Ethiopia in the west. For climatic reasons the Chinese preferred to wear shoes, and by the fifth century they had expanded the big-toe stirrup into the foot stirrup. Muslim armies in Iran received the stirrup in A.D. 694, and it reached the Franks about 730. The stirrup was the most important

[9]

military invention prior to gunpowder. Previously a mounted warrior could wield a lance only with the strength of his arm; now he could lay it under his right arm, and the blow was delivered by the weight of his charging steed. In the West the stirrup's arrival caused a miltary revolution. Charles Martel seized Church lands and distributed them to vassals on condition that they would stand ready to fight in the new, difficult and costly manner of mounted shock combat of which the stirrup was the essential element. For several generations this endowed feudal class was strictly military in its functions, but with the disintegration of the Carolingian power it began to become a governing class also. By the later twelfth century the rise of mercenary armies had largely destroyed its military utility, and by the middle of the thirteenth century the growth of the royal bureaucracies had ousted the feudal aristocracy in great part from their governmental functions as well, at least in western Europe. But meanwhile the feudal class had constructed an elaborate specialized culture called chivalry ("horsiness"). This ethos, centering around the original knightly obligation to do battle on horseback at the command of a liege lord, continued to dominate secular society in Europe for centuries more, because, despite their obsolescence, the aristocrats still enjoyed prestige and revenues. The arrival in the eighth century of the Chinese form of the Indic stirrup was basic to this entire development.[30]

Likewise, in the eighth century, Europe began to absorb improvements in the harnessing of horses which seem to have come from eastern or central Asia. Yoke-harness is efficient for oxen, but for anatomical reasons it is inappropriate to the horse. Even before the Han dynasty, the Chinese were experimenting with better forms of horse harness involving breast-straps and lateral shafts or traces. A few centuries later there are ambiguous pictures of different experiments with harness along the western frontiers of China, indicating perhaps that central Asia was the real center of innovation. Such ideas spread westward: on an Irish cross generally dated in the eighth century a breast-strap harness appears,[31] and a horse-collar with lateral traces is found in a Carolingian illumination of ca. 800.[32] With either of these new harnesses a team of horses can pull between four and five times the load possible with a yoke. The first evidence of the habitual use of horses in plowing comes from Norway in the late ninth century. By the end of the eleventh century horses were displacing oxen for agricultural labor over much of northern Europe, from the Channel to the Ukraine. Since horses are about twice as efficient as oxen, this substitution greatly increased the prosperity of the northern peasantry. The new harness, imported from Asia, helped notably to increase the food supply, population and urbanization of northern Europe in the Later Middle Ages. It also increased inland commerce by making possible large horse-drawn wagons.

The mechanical crank, which had been known in China since Han times, may also have been diffused to Europe at about this time. However, it is more probably a parallel Western invention, since its first European appearance, in the early ninth century, shows it applied to a rotary grindstone, and its second, about a hundred years later, attaches it to a hurdy-gurdy:[33] neither rotary grindstones nor hurdy-gurdies were used in China. Cultural diffusions at this time from eastern and central Asia to the Carolingian realm should not astonish us. Until the xenophobic reaction under Wu Tsung in 845, T'ang China was remarkably accessible to foreigners.

No further Western borrowings from Asia have been traced thereafter until the late tenth century, when chess and the fiddle-bow arrived through Muslim Spain. The fiddle-bow seems first to be found in eighth-century Java;[34] carried by the spice trade, it appears in the Islamic *rebāb* and in Spanish Christian illuminated manuscripts of about 980.[35] In Europe it achieved its greatest elaboration, culminating in the string quartet and the string section of the modern symphonic orchestra. Likewise at the end of the tenth century chess arrived, ultimately from India, apparently by the same route since the first evidence of the game in Latin Christendom is a legacy of chessmen in the will of a Count of Urgel in 1008. The game spread quickly in Europe and for some two hundred years was played with nearly identical rules from Greenland to the Indus. Thereafter innovations appearing in chess generally started in the West and spread eastward.[36]

Although cotton, sugar and rice had long been imported from India as luxuries, they were not cultivated on the shores of the Mediterranean until the Middle Ages. In the 970's ibn Hawqal mentions cotton growing in Tunisia; shortly afterward it is found in Sicily, and in the later twelfth century cotton plantations in Spain were using Sicilian methods.[37] Sugarcane follows an identical pattern.[38] As for rice, its cultivation was delayed: the rapid expansion of production in Valencia during the late thirteenth century seems to indicate a recent introduction, and it is not mentioned in Sicily before the same period. Its cultivation reached Pisa in 1468 and Lombardy in 1475.[39] Since in Thrace growing rice was at first a Muslim privilege which only later was opened to Christians, its introduction was presumably Turkish, and of the earlier fifteenth century.[40]

The eleventh century offers two curious items of European borrowing from farther Asia. The pointed arch and vault, as distinct from the catenary arch long employed in the Near East, originated primarily as a decorative form in Buddhist India. It appears in A.D. 836-876 in the Great Mosque of Sāmarrā, and immediately thereafter in the Mosque of ibn Tulūn in Cairo. By the early eleventh century pointed arches on the Fatimite pattern are found in the Old Cathedral of Amalfi, a city with many Egyptian connections at that time. Here the great Abbot Desiderius of Monte Cassino saw them, and the new church of his abbey, begun in 1066, was embellished with a porch of such arches and vaults. In 1083 Abbot Hugh of Cluny, already actively planning a vast new church at Cluny, visited Monte Cassino, with the result that the new abbey at Cluny, begun in 1088, contained 231 pointed arches and vaults which were used not only decoratively but also as a structural device for increasing the verticality of the thrust of the vaults and thus enabling the architect to raise them higher.[41] The new Cluny was the largest and most famous church of western Europe. In 1130 the Abbot of St. Denis, Suger, visited it. Then, between 1135 and 1144, Suger created at St. Denis the first "gothic" church, combining an ultimately Indian esthetic with an indigenous Frankish engineering invention.

At about the moment when the ogive was spreading from Amalfi, the legend of Gautama Buddha likewise began to percolate through the West. A version derived ultimately from the Sanskrit was known in Greek by the tenth century. In 1048 a western cleric resident in Greece put this into Latin under the title *Barlaam et Joasaph,*[42] the latter name being a corruption of *Bodhisattva.* The legend quickly spread through most of the vernaculars, and eventually Joasaph, or Buddha, was recognized as a saint in both the Greek and Latin churches, his feast day in the latter being November 27.

The twelfth century was a period of intensive borrowing from the farther Orient. Two Western innovations coming directly from China at that time warn us not to exaggerate the importance of the Crusades or to expect all diffusions from farther Asia to travel through the Near East; clearly, the caravan roads of central Asia could serve as an independent route. First, in 1004 a trebuchet operated by a gang of men pulling simultaneously on ropes appears in China. Slightly more than a century later this form of artillery is shown in a Spanish Christian manuscript, and in 1147 a battery of these trebuchets was used by northern Crusaders to capture Muslim Lisbon. Within the next few decades trebuchets in several forms are found all over Islam as well as Europe.[43] Second, by 1119 the Chinese were using the magnetic needle for navigation. In the last decade of the century it had reached Europe and by 1218 was common. Yet our first Muslim reference to it comes from Iran in A.D. 1232–3; it was still a novelty among the Arabs in 1282, and one of its Arabic names, *al-konbas,* indicates that it reached the Levant from the West, probably from Italy.[44] Clearly some borrowings from distant Asia were first effective in the Frankish regions and were diffused thence to the Near East. And perhaps some useful Chinese inventions, like the

[13]

wheelbarrow which appears in a Chartres window ca. 1220,[45] were never taken over in the Levant until modern times. Naturally, however, most Asian diffusions to the West were filtered through Islam and Byzantium. A remarkable example, which arrived in the twelfth century by two routes, is the Sanskrit *Pañcatantra*. In the sixth century it was translated into Pahlavi; from this, in turn, an eighth-century Arabic version was made, under the title *Kalila and Dimna,* which about 1080 served as the basis of a Greek edition. A hundred years later the famous Admiral Eugenios of the Norman court of Palermo sponsored a Greek text revised on the basis of the Arabic,[46] and these fables were then turned into Latin by a certain Baldo, otherwise unknown.[47] Meanwhile, about 1110, in his widely influential *Disciplina clericalis,* Petrus Alfunsi, an Arabic-speaking Jewish convert to Christianity, had already used many of the *Pañcatantra* materials taken directly from the Arabic version.[48] During the later Middle Ages these Indian animal stories spread through most of the European literatures.

Another pair of items arriving toward the end of the twelfth century were important for the eventual development of military organization in Europe. The transverse flute of China and India had reached the Mediterranean in Roman times but had not survived there. It came anew to Byzantium from the East ca. 800. The first Western evidence of it is in a German manuscript of 1205. In combination with another Oriental novelty, the double-ended drum, it began to provide marching music for the mercenary infantry of the rising monarchies.[49] Without some such technical device, the military drill and discipline which came to characterize European armies could not have developed.

The twelfth century was the chief period of the mediation of Indic science, through Arabic writings, to the West. The exact extent of this debt, however, cannot be ascertained at present because the central unsolved problem in the genetics of Islamic culture is the number and nature of the chromosomes which came from India: the turban is the symbol of this enigma.

In mathematics, however, a few things are certain. In A.D. 772, as part of a general program of translating Greek and Sanskrit works into Arabic, the Caliph al-Mansūr sponsored a version of one of the *Siddhāntas* which had been brought to Bagdad by a Hindu scholar. While such works were saturated with Hellenistic astronomy, they also contained original elements of importance, notably the sine.[50] Fifty years later the great mathematician al-Khwārizmī synthesized Greek and Indic mathematics. His work on arithmetic is not extant in Arabic but survives in a twelfth-century Latin version, *Algoritmi de numero indorum*. His algebra was put into Latin about the same time.[51] About A.D. 1000 Maslama al-Majrīti of Cordova had issued a revised version of al-Khwārizmī's astronomical tables which included not only the sine but also the tangent function—the latter possibly an addition by Maslama. In 1126 Adelard of Bath introduced Indian trigonometry, in this Arabic version, to the Latin West by means of a translation of these tables.[52] In 1149 Robert of Chester adapted the tables to the coordinates of London, and, in the course of revising Adelard's translation, introduced the Latin word *sinus*,[53] which through a series of mistranslations and transliterations is derived from the Sanskrit word for sine.[54] But even though the intellectual tools were now available, no further progress along this line was made until the first decades of the fourteenth century when, very suddenly, trigonometric ways of thinking surged forward in the works of the Provençal Jewish mathematician Levi ben Gerson and of a group centering at Merton College, Oxford.[55] It is evident that late medieval trigonometry, with all that it implies, depended on the twelfth-century diffusion of Indic concepts.

At the same moment the Indic number-system was penetrating the West. The idea of zero on a decimal base, and positional valuation of numerals, emerged in India before A.D. 600, probably from Babylonian sexagesimal sources,[56] and quickly percolated into Muslim mathematical methods. By the middle of the twelfth century, Latin translations of Arabic treatises made available to the West some knowledge of zero and its uses.[57] But the real appropriation of the system by Europe occurred in 1202 with the appearance of Leonardo Fibonacci of Pisa's *Liber abaci* which was designed to teach calculation "after the manner of the Indians." Fibonacci was no neglected genius: he was a conspicuous member of the court of Emperor Frederick II of Hohenstaufen. Within a few generations the novel numerical methods which he taught had penetrated all aspects of European commerce, government and science. It is difficult to picture the shape which Western culture would have assumed without this great gift of India. Incidentally, despite its intensive Eastern contacts, Byzantium did not begin to use the Indic arithmetic until 1252.[58]

The European contemporaries of Fibonacci were absorbing another concept from India which modern science considers fallacious, but which played a fundamental part in the development of the West: the idea of perpetual motion.[59] *Perpetua mobilia* first appeared ca. 1150 in the *Siddhānta śiromani* of Bhāskarā. The Muslims quickly appropriated the notion: an Arabic treatise associated with Ridwān's works of ca. A.D. 1200 contains six gravitational perpetual motion machines. One of these is identical with one of Bhāskarā's, while two of them are the same as the first two such devices to appear in Europe in Villard de Honnecourt's sketchbook of ca. 1235. A Latin work of the later fourteenth century describes a *perpetuum mobile* very like Bhāskarā's second proposal, while in the 1440's the Siennese engineer Jacopo Mariano Taccola presented a machine of radial hinged flails which is found in the Arabic treatise. We may therefore be confident that perpetual motion is an idea transmitted from India through Islam to Europe in the pontificate of Innocent III or shortly thereafter.

The characteristics of European interest in perpetual motion, in contrast to that in India and Islam, are the efforts to diversify the motor and to make it perform useful work. For example, inspired by the mariner's compass that, as we have seen, reached Europe from China in the 1190's, the military engineer Peter of Maricourt in 1269 proposed a magnetic *perpetuum mobile,* an automatically rotating armillary sphere that would displace all existing clocks. In the later thirteenth century European scientists and technicians began to regard the cosmos as a vast reservoir of energies waiting to be tapped in mankind's service. Friar Roger Bacon, Maricourt's friend, was vividly aware of the practical value of harnessing such forces. The Indic idea of perpetual motion, however false in itself, was a significant element in the late-medieval attitude toward the exploitation of nature which is the presupposition of modern power technology.

In the early thirteenth century a cluster of items with an emphatically Indic appearance surrounds the new mendicant orders authorized by Innocent III. The first was mendicancy itself. For the previous nine centuries and more, since the days of St. Pachomius, the vast majority of Christian ascetics, with amazing unanimity in theory and considerable constancy in practice, had insisted on the spiritual necessity of manual labor: it was a form of worship as obligatory as the *opus Dei* in the sanctuary. Then suddenly, shortly after 1200, a segment of Latin monasticism, the friars, abandoned this ancient Christian pattern of the religious life and adopted what appears to be the Brahmanic and Buddhist style of mendicant asceticism. Second, from their earliest years, the identifying sign of the Franciscans was a knotted cord around the waist. Tht world's religions are filled with symbolic cinctures, but these are generally assumed only for special rites. The closest analogy of the Franciscan cord is the sacred cord worn perpetually by the Brahmans as a sign of their identity. Third, at this same moment, and associated with the piety of the mendicant orders, the ancient gesture of prayer with outstretched arms was widely replaced in Europe by a new posture *junctis manibus*[60] that is identical with the *namaskara,* the Indic gesture of reverence and prayer. Fourth, shortly after the middle of the thirteenth century, and largely propagated by the friars, the Indic habit of using a string of beads for counting repetitions of prayers— a device adopted in Islam at least as early as the tenth century[61]

—swept Europe in the form of the paternoster.[62] Finally, the novel Franciscan attitude toward animals may be tinged with Indic metempsychosis—an hypothesis buttressed by the appearance of metempsychosis in the Provençal *Kabbala* about 1200.[63]

Each of these traits individually might be considered indigenous to Europe, but as a cluster they suggest a stream of Indic influences powerful in North Italy and Languedoc, the regions where both Dominicans and Franciscans achieved their formation. These were the parts of Europe in which Catharism, the chief challenge to the new Catholic mendicants, at that moment had its greatest growth. Although clear connections of the Western Cathars cannot now be traced further east than Constantinople, large communities of similar dualists long had flourished in central Asia in close conjunction with Buddhism. As late as the eleventh century they were still powerful in East Turkestan.[64] The Western Cathars believed in metempsychosis.[65] The clergy of the Bogomils, who seem to have dominated the Western heretics until the 1160's, were mendicants.[66] The clergy of the Western Cathars wore, as a sign of identity, a cord *supra camisam*.[67] The only prayer which the Cathar clergy ever said was the *Pater noster,* recited in units of sixteen repetitions, done fourteen times a day,[68] presumably with a counting device. We do not know the Cathar posture or prayer, but the Manichees of Turkestan, like their Buddhist neighbors, prayed *junctis manibus*.[69] The subject of possible Indic influences on the European friars demands further study.

It is usually assumed that after 1241 the Mongol conquests, by bringing political unity and relative safety for commerce to the entire land-mass from Poland to the Yellow Sea, opened a new era of contact between Europe and Asia which finds its chief symbol in Marco Polo, and that this period lasted until the Yuan dynasty was overthrown by the Mings in 1368. The records of travel confirm this hypothesis, but our inventory of European borrowings from the most distant parts of Asia shows neither increase nor decrease in volume for at least the first three generations of the Mongol Age. About 1250 a curious waterclock governed by a large wheel mounted on a horizontal axle is found at the Paris court of St. Louis. Its only analogy is the waterclock perfected in China in the late eleventh century.[70] The Chinese art of papermaking had been appropriated by Muslims at Samarkand in A.D. 751 after the capture of Chinese prisoners, and quickly spread to Mesopotamia and Syria. The first known Western document on paper is a Greek charter of Countess Adelasia of Sicily dated 1101–2,[71] but doubtless the paper was an import. The earliest paper factory in Latin Europe appears near Fabriano in 1276.[72] Another East Asian item of considerable importance not only for the textile industry but for the theory of machine design (because it incorporates cord drive) was the spinning wheel. It is found in China by 1035, and is mentioned at Speyer ca. 1280.[73] The spinning wheel, by notably increasing each spinner's production, cheapened thread and therefore reduced the cost of, and expanded the market for, plain cloth. One result was a vast increase of consumption of linen in the fourteenth century, "le siècle de la chemise." This produced vast quantities of linen rags which in turn probably lowered the cost of paper, thus adding an incentive toward the development of printing. Thus, in their new European context, quite different borrowings from further Asia joined to produce novel effects.

Gunpowder was known in China by 1040 and appears in Western Europe in the 1260's in firecrackers and rockets.[74] Since among the Arabs saltpetre was sometimes called "Chinese snow," the knowledge of gunpowder was probably diffused westward. The Chinese of the thirteenth century sometimes used what the West has called "Roman candles" shot from bamboo tubes as infantry weapons, but they did not yet propel missiles from metal tubes by means of gunpowder. The Byzantines, on the other hand, used bronze or brass tubes to project Greek fire.[75] Cannons appear in Europe by 1326,[76] and are first datable in China in 1332.[77] Considering the number of Italians in China in these decades, the diffusion may have gone in either direction. Since not only Islam and India but even Japan[78] received cannons from the West rather than from China, chemical artillery is probably a western European invention, on the basis of Chinese gunpowder and Byzantine military pyrotechnics.

Strangely, the fourteenth century offers little evidence of European borrowings from further Asia. The game of cards, of Chinese or Indic origin, emerges suddenly in the 1370's in various parts of Europe[79] and begins to displace the older Indic game of chess in popularity. Playing cards were produced by xylography, but since this ancient Indian technique had probably been applied in the West to textile printing since Roman times, the block-books which helped to prepare the way for Gutenberg's invention cannot be considered a recent diffusion from Asia.

Demonstrably south Asian cultural items reaching Europe in the fifteenth century are few. Following the spice trade, the blowgun had arrived in Italy from Indonesia before 1425, still carrying a form of its Malay name *sumpitan:* Arabic, *zabatāna,* Italian, *cerbottana.*[80] Air-guns were developed on the basis of the blowgun, and these, together with the suction pump, became the basis of the study of vacua and pressures which were so important for both science and engineering in the seventeenth century. Eventually we shall perhaps discover other south Asian traits introduced in this period to European folklore, tales, dance, music and metal crafts by the Gypsies, who entered the German lands from Hungary in 1407 and spread rapidly over western Europe.[81] The remarkable affinity with the Prakrit tongues observed in the archaic Romany dialect still spoken by the Gypsies of the Welsh mountains[82] shows that, despite their long wanderings, these tribes were still essentially Indic when they arrived in the West.

The later fourteenth and early fifteenth centuries likewise witnessed a massive influx of slaves from central Asia[83] to Italy and other areas of Genoese commerce. The Black Death of 1348–49 had created a shortage of labor. To meet the market, the Genoese trading posts on the Black Sea soon began to ship to the West many thousands of "Tartar" slaves gathered by Turkish slavers from as far as the regions north of Tibet and China.[84] This traffic probably accounts for the introduction of a few central Asian and east Asian items which appear in Europe in the first half of the fifteenth century. The "moulin turquoys à vent" mentioned in 1408,[85] may well be the vertical-axle windmill, common in Afghanistan and China, that is first pictured in Europe in the notebook of a Sienese engineer of 1438–50.[86] The related Chinese "helicopter" top which is the basis of Leonardo da Vinci's helicopter design, appears as *ludus pueri* in the same manuscript.[87] Buckwheat, sometimes called *turcicum frumentum,* a central Asian cereal, had reached Mecklenburg by 1436.[88] The Chinese water-powered trip-hammer, which contrasts sharply in design with the water-powered stamp-mill of Europe, emerges in the West about 1440 in the notebook of a German engineer who participated in the Hussite wars.[89] The importation of central Asian slaves was largely ended by the disruption of Genoese commerce resulting from the fall of Constantinople in 1453. For the latter part of the century only one new item seems to be a novelty from the East: a ball-and-chain governor for mills exactly analogous to that on the hand prayer-cylinder of Tibet. This is pictured in an Italian engineering manuscript of 1482–1501.[90]

Our inventory of traits that came to the West from India, China and central Asia during the Middle Ages should make historians distrustful of the adequacy of surviving written records. The extant documents would not lead us to expect the diffusions of the apparently Indic traits of the mendicants, or of the trebuchet and compass from China by channels independent of Islam. In contrast, the documented facilitation of travel following the Mongol conquests would lead us to anticipate subsequent borrowing at a pace that cannot be demonstrated: diffusions continued, but at a diminished rate. Yet even after Ming xenophobia had supposedly closed the gates of China to foreigners, a few Chinese items penetrated to Europe, although perhaps they arrived from the borderlands of China rather than from the Middle Kingdom directly. In any case, it is clear that the cultural history of Europe and of

NOTES

1. L. White, jr., *Medieval Technology and Social Change* (Oxford, 1962), pp. 34-35.

2. *Ibid.*, pp. 35-36, 151-52.

3. Li Ch'iao P'ing, *The Chemical Arts of Old China* (Easton, Penna., 1948), p. 181.

4. A. J. Arberry, *Classical Persian Literature* (London, 1958), p. 440; E. Rosen, "The Invention of Eyeglasses," *Journal of the History of Medicine and Allied Sciences*, XI (1956), 13-46.

5. Giovanni Dondi dall'Orologio, *Tractatus astrarii*, ed. A. Barzon et al. (Vatican, 1960), p. 27.

6. J. P. Peters, "The Cock," *Journal of the American Oriental Society*, XXXIII (1913), 363-96.

7. J. Schlosser, "Heidenische Elemente in der christlichen Kunst des Altertums," in *Präludien* (Berlin, 1927), p. 31; R. Pettazzoni, "The Pagan Origin of the Three-Headed Representation of the Christian Trinity," *Journal of the Warburg and Courtauld Institutes*, IX (1946), 135-51.

8. White, *Medieval Technology*, pp. 86-87, 161.

9. E. Wiedemann, "Die Konstruktion von Springbrunnen durch muslimische Gelehrte," in *Festschrift zur Feier des hundertjährigen Bestehens des Wetterauischen Gesellschaft für die gesamte Naturkunde zu Hanau* (Hanau, 1908), p. 36.

10. T. F. Carter, *The Invention of Printing in China and Its Spread Westward*, 2nd ed. (New York, 1955), p. 240.

11. É. Salin, *La civilisation mérovingienne*, III (Paris, 1957), 257.

12. G. Jacob, *Arabische Berichte von Gesandten an germanische Fürstenhöfen aus dem 9. und 10. Jahrhunderts* (Berlin, 1927), p. 31.

13. R. Hennig, "Indienfahrten abendländischer Christen im frühen Mittelalter," *Archiv für Kulturgeschichte*, XXV (1935), 275.

14. S. D. Goithein, "Letters and Documents on the India Trade in Medieval Times," *Islamic Culture*, XXXVII (1963), 188–205.

15. Matthew Paris, *Chronica majora*, ed. H. R. Luard (London, 1872–84), III, 161, and V, 340–41; G. Soulier, "Le moine arménien Hethoum et les apports d'Extrême-Orient à la fin du XIIIe et au commencement du XIVe siècle," *Revue des études arméniennes*, X (1929), 249–54.

16. "Itineraria et relationes fratrum minorum saeculi XIII et XIV," ed. A. Van den Wyngaert in *Sinica franciscana*, I (Quaracchi, 1929), 460.

17. R. S. Lopez, "Nuove luci sugli italiani in Estremo Oriente prima di Colombo," in *Studi colombiani* (Genoa, 1952), III, 337–98.

18. C. Trasselli, "Un italiano in Etiopia nel XV secolo: Pietro Rambulo da Messina," *Rassegna di studi etiopici*, I (1941), 179–80.

19. *A Genovese in India in the Fifteenth Century: Account of the Journey of Hieronimo di Santo Stefano* (London, 1857), p. 8.

20. Salin, *La civilisation mérovingienne*, IV (Paris, 1959), 498.

21. *Excavations at Helgö, I: Report for 1954–56*, ed. W. Holmquist (Stockholm, 1961), p. 112, pl. 21,22.

22. R. Bernheimer, *Romanische Tierplastik* (Munich, 1931), pp. 98–99; G. C. Druce, "The Elephant in Medieval Legend and Art," *Archaeological Journal*, LXXVI (1919), 65.

23. L. White, jr., "Tibet, India and Malaya as Sources of Western Medieval Technology," *American Historical Review*, LXV (1960), 517.

Lynn White, jr.

24. H. and R. Kahane and A. Tietze, *The Lingua Franca in the Levant: Turkish Nautical Terms of Italian and Greek Origin* (Urbana, 1958), p. 272.

25. L. Boulnois, *The Silk Road* (London, 1966), p. 138.

26. R. S. Lopez, "The Silk Industry in the Byzantine Empire," *Speculum*, XX (1945), 1–42.

27. F. Chalandon, *Histoire de la domination normande en Italie et en Sicile* (Paris, 1907), II, 136–37, 703–704.

28. *Cambridge Economic History of Europe*, ed. M. Postan et al. (Cambridge, Eng., 1952), II, 265. W. Hensel and L. Leciejewicz, "En Pologne médiévale: l'archéologie au service de l'histoire," *Annales: économies, sociétés, civilisations*, XVII (1962), 220, report the cocoon of a silk worm found at Poznan in a stratum of the late tenth century.

29. Paulus Diaconus, *Historia Langobardorum*, ed. G. Waitz (Hannover, 1878), p. 150; V. Hehn, *Kulturpflanzen und Haustiere in ihrem Übergang aus Asien nach Greichenland und Italien sowie das übrige Europa*, 9th ed. (Hildesheim, 1963), pp. 477–78.

30. White, *Medieval Technology*, pp. 1–38.

31. C. Singer et al., *A History of Technology*, II (Oxford, 1956), 544, fig. 490.

32. White, *Medieval Technology*, p. 61, pl. 3.

33. *Ibid.*, p. 110.

34. M. Hood, "The Effects of Medieval Technology on Musical Style in the Orient," in *Selected Reports of the Institute of Ethnomusicology, University of California, Los Angeles*, I (1970), pp. 147–70.

35. C. Sachs, *A History of Musical Instruments* (New York, 1940), p. 275.

36. J. R. Murray, *A History of Chess* (Oxford, 1913), pp. 413–14, 394.

37. M. Amari, *Storia dei musulmani di Sicilia*, ed. C. A. Nalino (Catania, 1935), II, 509–12.

38. *Ibid.*, II, 509.

39. *Cambridge Economic History*, I, 137.

40. F. Babinger, "Die Aufzeichnungen des Genuesen Jacopo de Promontorio-de Campis über den Osmanenstaat um 1475," *Bayerische Akademie der Wissenschaften, phil.-hist. Kl., Sitzungsberichte* (1956), VIII, 65, n. 3.

41. K. J. Conant, "The Pointed Arch: Orient to Occident," *Palaeologia* (Osaka), VII (1957), 33–36.

42. P. Peeters, "La prèmiere traduction latine de 'Barlaam et Joasaph' et son original grec," *Analecta bollandiana*, XLIX (1931), 276–312.

43. White, *Medieval Technology*, pp. 102, 165.

44. *Ibid.*, p. 132.

45. J. Needham, *Science and Civilisation in China*, IV, Part 2 (Cambridge, Eng., 1965), 258. The case for diffusion is probable but not certain. The Chinese wheelbarrow places the load on each side of a central wheel; the Western form places the load between the worker and an anterior wheel which may, therefore, be simply a substitute for the front man in the earlier hand barrow.

46. L. O. Sjöberg, *Stephanites und Ichnelates* (Studia graeca upsaliensia, 2; Uppsala, 1962), pp. 108–109.

47. A. Hilke, "Ein lateinische Übersetzung der greichischen Version des Kalila-Buchs," *Abhandlungen der Gessellschaft der Wissenschaften zu Göttingen, Phil.-hist. Kl.*, Neue Folge, XXI, iii (1928), 59–166.

48. H. Schwarzbaum, "International Folklore Motifs in Petrus Alfonsi's *Disciplina clericalis*," *Sefarad*, XXI (1961), 267–99; XXII (1962), 17–59, 321–44; XXIII (1963), 54–73.

49. Sachs, *History of Musical Instruments*, pp. 287–90.

50. G. Sarton, *Introduction to the History of Science*, I (Baltimore, 1927), 387.

51. *Ibid.*, p. 563.

52. H. Suter, *Die astronomischen Tafeln des Muhammad ibn Mūsā al-Khwārizmī in der Bearbeitung des Maslama ibn Ahmed al-Majrītī und der lateinische Übersetzung des Athelard von Bath* (Copenhagen, 1914).

53. C. H. Haskins, *Studies in the History of Mediaeval Science*, 2nd ed. (Cambridge, Mass., 1927), p. 123.

54. H. Hankel, *Zur Geschichte der Mathematik in Altertum und Mittelalter*, 2nd ed. (Hildesheim, 1965), pp. 280–81.

55. Sarton, *History of Science*, III (1947), 116–17, 129.

56. O. Neugebauer, *The Exact Sciences in Antiquity*, 2nd ed. (Providence, 1957), pp. 18–27, 166–89.

57. K. Menninger, *Zahlwort und Ziffer* (Göttingen, 1958), II, 226–27.

58. Sarton, *History of Science*, II (1931), 973.

59. White, "Tibet," pp. 522–26.

60. G. B. Ladner, "The Gestures of Prayer in Papal Iconography of the Thirteenth and Early Fourteenth Centuries," in *Didascaliae: Studies in Honor of Anselm M. Albareda*, ed. S. Prete (New York, 1961), pp. 247–75.

61. J. Goldziher, "Le rosaire dans l'Islam," *Revue de l'histoire des religions*, XXI (1890), 295–300.

62. T. Esser, "Zur Archäologie der Paternoster Schnur," in *Compte rendu du quatrième Congrès Scientifique International des Catholiques* (Frieburg, 1898), I, 338–74.

63. G. G. Scholem, *Ursprung und Anfänge der Kabbala* (Berlin, 1962), pp. 168–71.

64. A. von Le Coq, *Manichaica* (Berlin, 1922), III, 40.

65. H. Söderberg, *La religion des Cathares* (Uppsala, 1949), pp. 152–54.

66. A. Borst, *Die Katharer* (Stuttgart, 1953), p. 188.

67. C. Schmidt, *Histoire et doctrine de la secte des Cathares ou Albigeois* (Paris, 1848), II, 127, n. 7.

68. Borst, *Die Katharer*, pp. 190–92.

69. A. von Le Coq, *Chotscho* (Berlin, 1913), Taf. 3b.

70. Needham, *Science and Civilization*, IV, Part 2, 543; White, *Medieval Technology*, pp. 120–21, pl. 10.

71. E. Caspar, *Roger II* (Innsbruck, 1904), pp. 482, 561.

72. A. Zonghi, "Le antiche carte fabrienesi," in *Zonghi's Watermarks*, Vol. III of *Monumenta chartae papyraceae historiam illustrantia*, ed. E. J. Labarre (Hilversum, 1960), p. 114.

73. Needham, *Science and Civilization*, pp. 105, 758.

74. White, *Medieval Technology*, p. 97.

75. J. R. Partington, *History of Greek Fire and Gunpowder* (Cambridge, Eng., 1960), pp. 18–19.

76. C. M. Cipolla, *Guns and Sails in the Early Phase of European Expansion, 1400-1700* (London, 1965), pp. 21, 32.

77. L. C. Goodrich, "Early Cannon in China," *Isis*, LV (1964), 193–95.

78. D. M. Brown, "The Impact of Firearms on Japanese Warfare," *Far Eastern Quarterly*, VII (1948), 236–53.

79. C. P. Hargrave, *History of Playing Cards* (Boston, 1930), *passim*.

80. White, "Tibet," p. 521–22.

81. D. M. M. Bartlett, "Münster's *Cosmographia universalis*," *Journal of the Gypsy Lore Society*, XXXI (1952), 83–90.

82. J. Sampson, *The Dialect of the Gypsies of Wales* (Oxford, 1926).

83. I. Origo, "The Domestic Enemy: The Eastern Slaves in Tuscany in the Fourteenth and Fifteenth Centuries," *Speculum,* XXX (1955), 321–66.

84. V. Lazzari, "Del traffico e delle condizioni degli schiavi in Venezia nei tempi di mezzo," *Miscellanea di storia italiana,* I (1862), 470.

85. L. Delisle, *Études sur la condition de la classe agricole en Normandie au moyen âge* (Evreux, 1851), p. 518, n. 35.

86. White, "Tibet," p. 519.

87. L. Reti, "Helicopters and whirligigs," *Raccolta vinciana,* fasc. XX (1964), 331–38.

88. Hehn, *Kulturpflanzen,* 513.

89. Needham, *Science and Civilization,* IV, Part 2, 395.

90. White, "Tibet," p. 520.

II

Twelfth-Century Spirituality and the Late Middle Ages

Giles Constable
Harvard University

It is now forty years since Lucien Febvre argued in a provocative article that the question of the causes of the Reformation and its origins in France had been badly put by historians.[1] The Reformation, he said, was a chapter not in the history of the Church, nor of theology, nor of a national state, but in the history of religion. It was "the sign and product of a profound revolution of religious sentiment," a search for a religion better suited to the age;[2] and it must be studied in relation to the social, economic, and political conditions of the late Middle Ages.[3] The success or failure of a religious movement depends more upon considerations of this sort than upon the innovations of its leaders or the weaknesses of the institutions against which it may be directed.[4] Historians should therefore concentrate less upon individual reformers than upon (in the words of William James) "the adequacy of their message to the mental needs of a large fraction of mankind."[5] Religious sentiments, however, are harder to study than theological positions or institutional structures. "The only sound plan," said James, "if we are ourselves outside the pale of such emotions, is to observe as well as we are able those who feel them, and to record faithfully what we observe."[6]

For the late Middle Ages, the field of observation includes not only a wide range of religious literature but also a variety of liturgical practices, pious devotions, and artistic sources which reflect the spiritual (as contrasted with the mental) state of late medieval man. Religious needs and feelings differ from period to period, region to region, and person to person,[7] and it is only by studying a mass of individual instances that a general picture of the spirituality of the age can be put together. Such a picture for the fifteenth century would emphasize the emotionalism, anti-intellectualism, and sensuousness which can be seen in the religious feelings of sadness, tenderness, and devotion to the human Christ, His mother Mary, and the saints. "A man will know God in so far as he loves Him," said the great popular preacher Bernardino of Siena. "A man knows as much as he loves." St. Paul taught not that men should understand Christ, according to Bernardino, but that they should feel within themselves as He felt on the cross and participate in His sufferings.[8] Men were thus driven to the complementary extremes of religious introversion and extroversion. The stress on inner experience promoted an intense search for personal perfection, culminating in self-annihilation and abandonment in mystical union with God. At the same time, men sought to demonstrate their devotion. The ferment of popular prophecy and millenarianism roused them to a sense of public urgency and extravagant emotional displays, which are considered by some scholars to show the malaise of society at that time. The flagellants, the dance frenzies, and the witch hunts can be seen as the growing pains of modern society and as signs of deep feelings of guilt and hostility. Ladner described the fifteenth-century witch hunts as "a condemnation of alienated people by other alienated people."[9] Psychic epidemics like the dance frenzies, said Rosen in his recent book, *Madness in Society,* were "closely linked with religious ritual and institutions" and were fundamentally "attempts to manage stressful situations."[10] The fool replaced the pilgrim as the "ruling idea" of society and the type of Christian man, and "for the first time in Christian history," as Ladner put it, "there were let loose in full force the vast potentialities of man's alienation from man."[11]

Even intellectuals, to many of whom such phenomena were

profoundly distasteful, shared the emphasis on inwardness and will of the popular religious movements. For Gerson, as for Bernardino, God is known in this life more by the affective than by the cognitive powers. In his second lecture *Contra curiositatem studientium* he maintained that, "A clear and wise understanding of those things which are believed from the Gospel, which is called mystical theology, should be acquired by penance rather than by human investigation alone."[12] Valla argued in his *De professione religiosorum* that goodness must be freely willed by men and asserted in his *De libero arbitrio* that, "We stand by faith, not by the probability of reasons."[13] And Pico in his commentary on the Psalms emphasized that inner piety is more important than external worship.[14] "This humanist approach to theology may be traced from Petrarch to Erasmus," said Kristeller, who stressed that it influenced Protestants like Luther, Melanchthon, and Calvin as well as Catholics.[15] Even heretics, as Grundmann has shown, participated in this continuum of religious attitudes and often carried to extremes tendencies which in their more moderate manifestations were perfectly orthodox.[16]

Taken together, therefore, these elements characterized the spirituality of the late Middle Ages and must be seen as the product of complex forces at work in society at that time. Individually, however, many of these attitudes and devotions were far from new and can be found in the religious feelings and actions of much earlier Christians. The piety of the early Middle Ages was, indeed, not generally marked by emotionalism or extravagance, though individual instances can be cited, nor by popular devotion to the humanity of Christ, of which the suppression, according to some scholars, was a result of the reaction to Arianism.[17] Historians in recent years have increasingly regarded the late eleventh and twelfth centuries as the turning point in medieval spirituality, when the features which marked its later development first emerged.

The pioneer of this point of view was the textual scholar André Wilmart, who argued against Émile Mâle's opinion that there was a great difference between the religious spirits of the twelfth and fifteenth centuries. "It is the splendor of the twelfth century . . . ," Wilmart said, "to have discovered in the heart of Christianity veins that had not yet been exploited. . . . In most fields, thought, piety, art, literature, the twelfth century accomplished new work, extraordinarily fecund, and . . . truly inaugurated a distinct era in the history of Christian civilization."[18] A few pages later he went on:

> The Christianity of the eleventh century at times resembles that of the fourteenth and fifteenth centuries in a remarkable way. Even more, the forms of piety of the twelfth century are close to those that appeared later. It was not entirely with St. Francis and under the influence of St. Francis, as M. Mâle still asserts, that the devout, sensitive, and pathetic Middle Ages really took shape. Before him, St. Bernard and his Cistercian disciples are evidence of the new spirit. And already men of the previous generation, such as John of Fécamp and St. Anselm, anticipated the changes which were to appear.[19]

These views have been echoed and developed by Gilson, Chenu, Javelet, and especially Southern, who in his well-known book, *The Making of the Middle Ages,* emphasized the novelty in the eleventh and twelfth centuries of "the new type of ardent and effusive self-disclosure," the stress on personal experience and individual conscience, and "the theme of tenderness and compassion for the sufferings and helplessness" of Christ.[20]

In a recent article on the popularity of twelfth-century spiritual texts in the late Middle Ages, I have tried to indicate some of the links between the religious feelings of the two periods. The number of manuscripts, for example, shows that interest in these works, which fell off in the thirteenth and early fourteenth centuries, revived in the fifteenth and early sixteenth centuries. This is confirmed by the evidence of translations, library catalogues, recommended reading lists, and early printed editions. "The demand for the mystical Christian writers was so compelling in the period 1450–1550," wrote Goldschmidt in his book, *Medieval Texts and their First Appearance in Print,* "that it resulted in the publication of practically every work in this class which we now consider to be of importance and value."[21] Among the eleventh- and twelfth-century writers whose works were printed at this time were Adam of St. Victor, Amadeus of Lausanne, Anselm, Bernard (of whose works alone there were over five hundred editions printed before 1550[22]), Bruno, Elizabeth of Schönau, Guigo I and II of La Chartreuse, Hildegard of Bingen, Hugh of Fouilloy, Hugh of St. Victor, Innocent III, Joachim of Flora, John of Fécamp, Peter Damiani, Peter the Venerable, Richard of St. Victor, and William of St. Thierry, in addition to some minor and anonymous writers whose works circulated under the names of Augustine, Anselm, Bernard, and Hugh.

An interesting study could be written on the influence of almost every one of these writers. Bernard in particular enjoyed an enormous success in the late Middle Ages, when his influence has been compared by several scholars to that of Augustine. Bremond in his history of French religious sentiment in the seventeenth century spoke of Bernard as "that extraordinary man off whom we live today at least as much as we live off St. Augustine."[23] In the late Middle Ages he was admired by men of very different religious temperaments and theological beliefs, who found in his life and works spiritual attitudes and themes which appealed to their deepest religious inclinations. Not far behind Bernard in popularity and influence were Anselm, Hugh and Richard of St. Victor, and Joachim, whose contribution to the prophetic speculations of the fifteenth and sixteenth centuries has only begun to be investigated. Even minor, and today almost forgotten, twelfth-century works, like the *Speculum monachorum* of Arnulf of Bohéries and the *Scala claustralium* of Guigo II of La Chartreuse, were widely read.[24] Some of these texts are found only in late medieval manuscripts and thus owe not only their success but also their preservation to the devotional spirit of that age.

It is easier to establish the fact of than the reason for the popularity and influence of these works in late medieval intellectual and religious circles. Their success clearly depended not only on certain common qualities in the spirituality of the fifteenth century but also on an affinity of religious temperament between this age and the twelfth century. This affinity was not necessarily the result of any direct or conscious influence of the earlier on the later period, but it helps account for the popularity of its writings. Men in the late Middle Ages found certain congenial religious ideas and attitudes expressed in twelfth-century spiritual texts. Such works might either have been read continuously or have been lost sight of for years until they were rediscovered and appreciated, sometimes under attributions that entirely hid their true origins. Thus the period of the Renaissance, in its broadest sense, involved the reemphasis on and recombination of elements from the medieval as well as the classical traditions.[25] My main concern in this lecture will be with those elements found in twelfth-century spiritual texts and used by men in the late Middle Ages.

Above all they found an inward-looking and affective piety based on a doctrine of contemplation stressing personal will, liberty, and experience. When Renaudet said that d'Ailly and Gerson were "the heirs of St. Bernard and the Victorines," he had in mind their view of the contemplative life. D'Ailly owed to Richard, according to Renaudet, his description of the three classic stages of the spiritual life—purification, illumination, and union—and to Bernard his efforts to find in the Song of Songs the symbols of the love of the soul for Christ.[26] Gerson's definition of contemplation also depended primarily on Hugh and Richard, as Combes has shown in his recent study on the evolution of Gerson's mystical theology.[27] From them he learned the spiritual content of various biblical texts. More specifically, Gerson took from Richard and from Gilbert of Hoyland his teaching on violent love and from Bernard and William of St. Thierry his ideal of the "ambidextrous" prelate who combines in his own life both action and contemplation.[28] In the works of Hugh, said Roger Baron, Gerson, the writers of the school of the *Devotio moderna,* and other late medieval mystics found in germ "the mysticism of introversion, the theory of mystical passivity under divine action, [and] the conception of the soul as a mirror associated with the doctrine of the divine image of the soul."[29] The author of *The Cloud of Unknowing* "was probably indebted to Richard of St. Victor for the systematization of the way to contemplative prayer, some of his allegorical interpretations of Scripture, and possibly for the prevailing antithetical nature of his prose."[30] And through the *Explanacio* of Thomas Gallus, Richard is said by Javelet to have inspired the anti-intellectualist current in south German monasteries in the fifteenth century.[31] The mystical theology of Nicholas of Cusa, and especially his view of the powers of human reason, were influenced by Bernard and the Victorines. He found in their works, and even more, as Klibansky has shown, in the works of the twelfth-century masters at Chartres, many of the Platonic views for which he was famous among his contemporaries and which deeply influenced the development of Renaissance Platonism.[32]

The humanists no less than the theologians appreciated an emphasis on will and inner piety. Their dislike of scholastic intellectualism and speculative mysticism is well known. Valla, for instance, attacked Aquinas not only for his barbarous Latin but also for his logic and metaphysics.[33] And the early Christian fathers appealed to the humanists as much for their piety and scholarship as for their classical style.[34] The humanist attitude towards the twelfth century was on the whole less favorable, but the reaction against scholasticism inclined them to look with interest at pre-scholastic spirituality. Even Petrarch, who has been called the founder of the concept of the Dark Ages,[35] read with sympathy the works of Abelard, Hugh, Richard, and Bernard, to whom he devoted an admiring chapter in his *De vita solitaria*.[36] Petrarch's religious tracts, said Kristeller, "show some connection with the popular religious literature of the Middle Ages;"[37] and his spirituality, like his scholarship,[38] may have owed more to the twelfth century than he himself fully realized. The fact that the fifteenth-century humanist Pier Candido Decembrio derived much of his treatise on the immortality of the soul from the twelfth-century Cistercian treatise *De spiritu et anima*, which he believed to be by St. Augustine, also suggests that the religious outlook of the humanists had points in common with that of the twelfth century.[39]

An active interest in twelfth-century spiritual texts was shown in particular by the humanist circle of Lefèvre d'Étaples at Paris in the late fifteenth and early sixteenth centuries. The importance for this group of the idea of Christian antiquity has been studied by Eugene Rice, who said that, "The fathers offered Lefèvre and his friends a Christian vision of antiquity, a Christian eloquence, a Christian philosophy and an 'ancient and true theology.' "[40] In addition to the works of the Church fathers, however, they read and published a large number of medieval texts.[41] Lefèvre edited in 1513 a volume of various medieval spiritual writers, including Elizabeth of Schönau and Hildegard of Bingen, and in 1510 the *De trinitate* by Richard of St. Victor, in whose works he found, according to Renaudet, "in its entirety the rational and mystical theology for which he had ceaselessly searched."[42] Clichtove edited the works of Hugh of St. Victor, Hugh of Fouilloy, and Bernard, whom he praised in his introductory letter to the edition of 1508 for his elegant style, biblical learning, and sanctity of life.[43]

These works contain more than simply a definition of contemplation and a description of its principles. Some of the most original and important contributions of twelfth-century spirituality lay in its teachings on the psychology of the religious life and the importance of intention, liberty, self-knowledge, and love. Abelard, for instance, though he is not primarily known as a spiritual writer, influenced almost all subsequent teaching on morality by his emphasis on the significance of intention in human acts.[44] Both Hugh of St. Victor and Peter Lombard, who can hardly be described as disciples of Abelard, accepted his view that the merit of exterior actions depends on *intentio* and *voluntas,* though they rejected his opinion that all human acts are in themselves morally indifferent. This marked a revolution in moral doctrine, as Lottin has shown, and a reaction from the early medieval morality which defined sin as objective opposition to divine law and virtue as exterior observance of the law, especially in the framework of monastic life. The twelfth century saw the emergence of a more subjective and individual concept of virtue, which was closely related to the voluntarism of its spirituality.

Virtue of this sort must be chosen rather than imposed;[45] and the twelfth century was deeply concerned with the problem of liberty, though it had comparatively few new ideas on free will.[46] The biblical *locus classicus* was Paul's assimilation of liberty with the spirit of the Lord in 2 Corinthians 3.17, and the many twelfth-century references to "the spirit of liberty" and "liberty of the spirit" foreshadowed the emphasis on spiritual liberty in the religious thought of the late Middle Ages.[47] In a characteristic passage from a letter concerning novices, the Cistercian abbot Adam of Peresigne first cited Paul, "Where the spirit of the Lord is, there is liberty," and Bernard, "liberty, I say, from sin, from need, from misery," and then went on, playing with the reference to novelty in the term "novice," to say that, "The spirit is sent forth by God, morals are re-created, the face of the earth is renewed [a reference to Psalm 103.30], and you can rejoice in your novices, since the power from above makes them participants in this marvellous innovation."[48] Adam's stress on the reform and re-creation of man shows the far-reaching implications of this concept of liberty for the standards of individual behavior in relation to established laws and institutions.

The individual Christian was increasingly expected to rely on himself and his own experience. "The urge towards a greater measure of solitude," wrote Southern, "of introspection and self-knowledge which is exemplified by St. Anselm in the bosom of the Benedictine order in the eleventh century ran like fire through Europe in the generation after his death and produced an outburst of meditations and spiritual soliloquies."[49] It is no accident that the alternate title of Abelard's *Ethics* is the Socratic maxim *Scito te ipsum*. Abelard, Bernard, William of St. Thierry, Hugh, and Richard all taught that self-knowledge was man's start on his way to God. The importance of this idea for later spirituality and philosophy need not be emphasized. Parallels have been seen with Pascal, and Adam of Dryburgh's "Scio me esse" is said to have been a link between Augustine and Campanella, Descartes, and the modern notion of individual consciousness as the basic fact of experience.[50] The orientation was naturally different in the Middle Ages, when self-consciousness was seen as a prelude to a vision of eternity rather than as a scientific methodology; but it marked an important shift in man's way of looking at himself and his spiritual life.

Above all, it contributed to a new view of the dignity and nobility of man, as a function of his liberty and rationality and as an aspect of his creation in the image of God.[51] Richard of St. Victor expressed this in his description in the *Benjamin major* of the first grade of contemplation: "A man's own experience can easily teach anyone, I think, how greatly this speculation [of the self and others] has power to arouse the soul both against sin and towards good. Recognize your dignity, oh man, I beg; consider the excellent nature of your soul, how God made it in His image and likeness, how He raised it above all bodily creatures."[52] Here in a few lines from one of the most widely read works of twelfth-century spirituality are found many elements of its dynamic and forward-looking message, which offered to all men the hope of reform into the image of God.[53]

An essential part of this message, and one that appealed strongly to the emotionalism of the late Middle Ages, was its emphasis on love. *Dilige et fac quod vis*—"Love and do what you will"—was a favorite maxim of this age.[54] It derived from Augustine's commentary on the epistles of John and meant that men who love rightly will behave rightly. For men in the twelfth century it was an expression of their voluntarist and God-centered piety, but it held the seeds of more radical sentiments. William James (who knew of its use, I think, only in post-Reformation sources) called it an "antinomian saying" and "morally one of the profoundest of observations, yet . . . pregnant . . . with passports beyond the bounds of conventional morality."[55] It emphasized the direct relation between the individual and God and prepared the way for the late medieval heretical belief that anyone filled with the love of God can perform no sinful action and may therefore freely indulge his natural inclinations.

Some traces of this attitude of abandonment to God are found in the late twelfth and early thirteenth centuries. Caesarius of Heisterbach, for instance, tells of a Cistercian monk who attributed his power to work miracles to his trust in God. "I do not pray, nor fast, nor keep vigils, nor work more than the other brothers," he said when questioned by his abbot, "but I know one thing: that prosperity cannot raise me up nor adversity cast me down. . . . I have committed myself totally to God. . . . And the abbot recognized that the cause of this power was the love of God and the contempt for worldly things."[56] The context here is entirely orthodox, as it was in much of later medieval mysticism, but the idea of total commitment to God, even when based on *amor Dei* and *contemptus mundi*, led towards the extreme views of impeccability and deification. Perfect love and poverty were for some medieval heretics the same as total liberty and annihilation.[57] Gerson in one of his sermons even warned against the doctrine of contemplation found in William of St. Thierry's *Golden Letter* owing to his fear of the view that a living person could be entirely lost in union with God.[58]

This subjective emphasis of twelfth-century spirituality can also be seen in the development of the view, based on Romans 3.28, that a man is justified by faith without the works of the law. In his first sermon on the feast of the Annunciation, Bernard maintained that "the testimony of our conscience," which St. Paul called "our glory" in 2 Corinthians 1.12, consisted of the three beliefs that sins are forgiven only by God, that good works are the gift of God, and that eternal life must be freely given by God. No one can have good works by himself, Bernard said, citing Romans 3.28, and no one should even believe that merits can be had except by faith until he has received testimony from the Holy Spirit that he has them by faith. "So also concerning eternal life you must have the testimony of the Spirit that you will attain it by divine aid."⁵⁹ This is a justly celebrated passage, but not unique in the twelfth century. Similar views were expressed by Isaac of L'Étoile and in an anonymous Cistercian treatise *De conscientia,* where the author said that God's unknowable and incomprehensible judgment justifies man by knowing his will, "which is the cause of salvation and damnation." He wrote, citing 2 Corinthians 1.12, "A man filled with God calls his conscience his glory, as if, fully perceiving it, he [were] also in it."⁶⁰ "This is the true glory, the indwelling glory," said Bernard, "since it is from Him who dwells by faith in our hearts."⁶¹

This is faith in the sense that William James defined it: a state of mind of which the glowing center is "a passion of willingness, of acquiescence, of admiration." It was at the same time a joyous and affective experience and a reassuring state of security for those who felt a need to surrender and to give up their constant activity and vigilance.⁶² This also was faith in Luther's sense of the term, and it is not surprising that Bernard's first sermon on the Annunciation has been considered by some scholars the inspiration of Luther's teaching on justification by faith.⁶³

The question of Luther's attitude towards Bernard has been much debated by both Catholic and Protestant historians and is mentioned here on account of the light it throws on the attitude of the late Middle Ages towards twelfth-century religious thought. There is no doubt that Luther was greatly influenced by Bernard, possibly even more than by Augustine.⁶⁴ Some of his early works, especially his commentary on the Psalms, have been said to read almost like works by Bernard.⁶⁵ Though the strength of this influence later weakened, Luther always expressed a special regard for Bernard. "I venerate him above all other monks," he said in his *Table Talk,* calling him "very sincere."⁶⁶ He particularly admired Bernard's life and preaching,⁶⁷ and in his *De votis monasticis* he cited two passages from Bernard's *Vita* and commented that, "You see that these are the words of a most Christian bosom, which placed total trust in God, utterly despairing of his [own] works."[68] Catholic scholars have pointed out that Luther misinterpreted Bernard's use of the word *perdite* here and took what was in fact an expression of humility as evidence that Bernard trusted for his salvation in God rather than his monastic vows.[69] Protestants, on the other hand, have read into Bernard proto-Lutheran doctrines on the relation of the individual to God, on the role of Christ, on justification by faith, and on penance.[70]

It may be that there are parallels between Bernard and Luther on these points. It may also be, as Mousnier suggested, that an unconscious mental framework formed by Luther's religious personality, philosophical position, and intellectual background allowed him to absorb from Bernard only what his own sensibility and way of reasoning could assimilate.[71] Certainly after a period of almost four hundred years, neither Luther nor any of his contemporaries could enter fully into the thought-world of Bernard. The sympathy between them was based less on doctrines than on feelings, however: a common reliance on the heart, experience, and the Bible.[72] In spite of Luther's training as a nominalist and his dislike for late medieval speculative mysticism,[73] he shared the spiritual needs and preoccupations of the mystics, as Strohl pointed out, and he liked their piety.[74] Even if there was no direct connection between Bernard's sermon on the Annunciation and Luther's doctrine on justification, therefore, they express a similar spiritual attitude and are framed in similar biblical language; and Luther can be taken literally in his praise of Bernard's sincerity, faith in Christ, "most Christian bosom," and apostolic activity.

Luther also shared with Bernard, and with many twelfth-century spiritual leaders, a fierce zeal for reform based on man's inner will and freedom. His use of the famous motto that Christ was truth not custom,[75] which derived ultimately from St. Augustine, was paralleled in the eleventh and twelfth centuries by its use in the works of Gregory VII, Urban II, Ivo of Chartres, Gratian, and Hervé of Bourg-Dieu, who tried in his treatise *De correctione quorumdam lectionum,* on the model of the early Christians, to purge the liturgy of its corruptions and to return, as he said, to the "pure truth as it was promulgated from the beginning by the evangelists and prophets."[76] The form of the primitive church, especially as described in Acts 4.32–35, was repeatedly cited in the eleventh and twelfth centuries as the ideal Christian community and the model for the contemporary church.[77] This was again a favorite theme in the late Middle Ages, as Leff has emphasized in a recent article on "The Apostolic Ideal in Later Medieval Ecclesiology."[78] "Erasmus was fond of rebuking the superstition and intolerance of his own day by the example of the early church," said Bainton. "From him, probably Luther, and Melanchthon in a measure, and more especially Zwingli, learned this device for combating the church of Rome."[79]

Both ages likewise made use of direct criticism and satire in their battle for reform, and there is some evidence here of continuity in their efforts. Owst, for instance, cites a bitter censure of the clergy by Hugh of Fouilloy which was "familiar to generations of English preachers and sermon-audiences."[80] Satires against the vices of the curia, clerics, and monks became an established and influential literary genre in the twelfth century and were composed by many different types of writers.[81] This criticism formed "an important and complex chapter of medieval literature," according to Curtius, and was revived and used as a weapon against Rome by such reformers as John Bale in England and Luther's follower Matthias Flacius in Germany. "Many a text has escaped destruction," Curtius concluded, "for no other reason."[82]

In the twelfth century criticism was directed not only at monks as individuals but also, for almost the first time in the West since the fifth century, at monasticism as an institution. This was the result less of reforming zeal and satirical malice than of the spirituality of inwardness and will, which stressed the need for choice and decision rather than obedience and conformity and contributed to the emerging reassessment of the relative merits of a life spent in a monastery and a life spent in the world.[83] In the early Middle Ages, the superiority of monasticism over all other forms of life on earth was generally recognized, and contemplation and action were seen not (as they often are today) as two mutually exclusive types of life but as closely related parts of a single, monastic life: action was the ascetic battle against vice which both prepared the way for and provided relaxation from the ardors of contemplation. A "mixed" life with alternating periods of action and contemplation was the ideal of many twelfth-century spiritual writers. Whether the action took the form of ascetic exercises, manual labor, or, more rarely, pastoral and caritative work in the world, it was seen as part of the monastic life.

The validity of an active life spent primarily in the world was also discussed in the twelfth century, especially as part of the debate over the relative dignities of the secular and regular clergy. Many of the champions of action in this sense were found in the ranks of the regular canons. In the works of Arno of Reichersberg and Anselm of Havelberg, said Dereine, "We find for the first time in the history of Christian spirituality a developed theory in which a priority is reciprocally accorded to the two activities . . . and which prepared the way for the doctrine of a mixed life developed by Thomas Aquinas in the thirteenth century."[84] This was the beginning of the spirituality of action which asserted the superiority of clerical over monastic life. The cleric conquers the world by battle, said Gerhoh of Reichersberg, the monk by flight.[85] And the Premonstratensian Philip of Harvengt declared that, "To flee the world from the middle of Babylon and to be saved is as much safer as it is easier; but to be crowned victor in the middle of Babylon is as much grander as it is harder; so that monastic perfection, although commendable for merit, is considered as much lower as it is easier than clerical [perfection]."[86] Even Peter the Venerable, writing to dissuade his secretary from becoming a hermit, argued that he should be a hermit with his heart rather than his body. "The laurel of victory is given not to him who flees," Peter wrote, "but to him who remains, not

[41]

to him who falls but to him who resists, not to him who submits but to him who conquers."[87]

This type of meritorious activity was still considered, in the twelfth century, to be within the framework of either a monastic or clerical life, but it pointed the way towards accepting the validity of a lay life of secular action. An indication of this direction, and of the declining prestige of monasticism, can be seen in the positive valuation put on marriage, the accepted hallmark of the lay order. The sanctity of a properly established marriage or betrothal was universally recognized in the twelfth century. Both partners were regarded as having rights and responsibilities which could not be unilaterly breached even for such worthy ends as entering a monastery, going on a crusade, or preserving virginity or chastity.[88] This appreciation of the human as well as the social values of married life was reflected in the marriage mysticism of Bernard and the Cistercians, who applied it to the life of the spirit rather than the body. The pure and unselfish love of a man for his wife was compared by Bernard to the love of God. "Love is a great thing," he wrote, "but there are grades in it. The bride is at the top."[89] Isaac of L'Étoile also praised the bond of piety and human agreement between man and wife.[90] An unusual example of this attitude, and of the appreciation of human tenderness in the twelfth century, can be seen on a Romanesque tomb from Belval, showing a wife embracing her pilgrim-husband, possibly on the occasion of his return from a crusade.[91]

A monument such as this was hardly noticed in the late Middle Ages, of course, and there is no evidence that the works of regular canons like Gerhoh of Reichersberg and Philip of Harvengt were widely read, but they reflected a shift in values which later became very significant. "In many religious movements of the high and late Middle Ages," wrote Hans Baron, "there was a pronounced shift to moralism and action. This can be seen in the successive development from the Benedictine to the Franciscan orders, and from the isolation and contemplation of the mystic to the more practical and active piety encountered in the *Devotio Moderna.*[92] Elsewhere Baron studied this shift in the changing views of Cicero from "a teacher of misogyny and flight from active life" to an exponent of civic virtue and a combined life of action and contemplation.[93] Appreciation of lay life and its values, and opposition to monasticism, were connected threads in the spiritual life of the fifteenth century. Valla in his *Dialecticae disputationes* rejected the distinction between the active and contemplative lives and declared that contemplation is a type of action; and in his *De professione religiosorum* he denied that the monastic life was in any way intrinsically superior, or more highly rewarded in heaven, than other ways of life.[94] Émile Telle in his book on Erasmus and marriage emphasized the importance of anti-monasticism as "the primordial phenomenon of the Pre-Reformation" and the connection between Erasmus's hostility to monasticism and his "matrimonial cult," in which marriage was the foundation of a full humanist *philosophia Christi.*[95]

A similar point of view was expressed by theologians in terms which show more clearly their debt to the twelfth century. Gerson, for instance, owed to William of St. Thierry his ideal of the "ambidextrous" prelate. "In declaring that the prelate, as such, must be ambidextrous," wrote Combes, "the preacher [Gerson] summoned up and made his own a famous theme which, for him and doubtless all his contemporaries, went back to St. Bernard and signified the optimum equilibrium between the two functions of a single charity: the contemplation of truth and the truth of active charity."[96] Against those who defended the intrinsic superiority of monasticism, Gerson asserted the thesis, as Oberman put it, that, "Perfection is not an absolute static standard but is dynamically related to the circumstances of a particular individual. . . . Biel formulates this succinctly by stating that *every Christian in a state of grace is in a state of perfection.* The contemplative life may be the purer one; the active life is nevertheless more intense and fruitful."[97] There was a lively debate in the fifteenth century on the respective merits of the two lives, and even a monk like prior Bernard of Tegernsee argued in a treatise written in 1462 that contemplation, though theoretically superior, cannot and should not in practice be separated from action.[98]

The stress of the Protestant reformers on freely performed acts of love and their opposition to binding monastic vows were not without precedents, therefore, and drew on a strain of spirituality which emphasized inner attitudes rather than outer forms and which questioned the value of a life of total withdrawal from the world. Valla's hostility to monasticism in the *De professione religiosorum* was based on the view "that goodness springs from the free impulses of a will which is internally well-directed and not from outward obedience to obligations externally imposed."[99] Bernard himself held that self-denial was useless if it was imposed on an individual against his will,[100] and his famous description of himself as "a sort of modern chimaera, neither cleric nor layman" prefigured the ambidextrous ideal of the mixed life of action and contemplation.[101] Four centuries later the context was very different, and Luther's rejection of monasticism may in his own terms have been distinctive and original, as Lohse argued in his book on monasticism and the Reformation;[102] but it must also be seen in the light of a long tradition of reexamining the basic nature of Christian life and perfection.

In popular religious life this was paralleled by a new spirit in devotions and the liturgy which also went back to the eleventh and twelfth centuries.[103] This is well illustrated by the continued popularity of the prayers of St. Anselm, which marked on the one hand a reaction from the sober piety of the Carolingian age, as Southern said, and on the other "introduced a new note of personal passion, of elaboration and emotional extravagance, which anticipated some of the chief features of later medieval piety. . . . Anselm's prayers opened the way which led to the *Dies irae,* the *Imitatio Christi,* and the masterpieces of later medieval piety." "Opinions will differ about the desirability of this new point of departure," he continued later, "this new *via pietatis* sprinkled with many tears;

but that it is a main road through the religion of the later Middle Ages cannot be doubted."[104]

This was a road of the heart rather than the head. It stressed the emotions of love, tenderness, and sadness and showed itself in countless ways in the religious life of the fifteenth century. Of particular importance was the devotion to the humanity of Christ, which ran all the way from the theological and moral ideal of the imitation of Christ to the most humble manifestations of love for every aspect of His earthly life and body. "The theme of tenderness and compassion for the sufferings and helplessness of the Savior of the world was one which had a new birth in the monasteries of the eleventh century," wrote Southern, "and every century since then has paid tribute to the monastic inspiration of this century by some new development of the theme."[105] Christ's life was divided into stages for pious meditation each hour of the day;[106] and the practice of publicly adoring His body in the form of the consecrated elements started in the twelfth century with the liturgical ceremony of the elevation and was formally recognized by the institution of Corpus Christi day in 1264.[107] Popular interest in the Eucharist was also shown by the increasing number of recorded eucharistic miracles, of which the best-known example, illustrated by Raphael in the Vatican *stanze,* was the thirteenth-century miracle of Bolsena.[108] The number of references to the stigmata also grew in the twelfth and thirteenth centuries. St. Francis was the most celebrated, but probably not the first, example of this supreme sign of devotion to the sufferings of Christ. This was shown in more popular form by the devotions of the rosary[109] and the Sacred Heart, of which Schreiber has traced the origins to the Premonstratensian abbey of Steinfeld, where the first known hymn to the Sacred Heart was composed in the second half of the twelfth century.[110]

The attribution to Christ of feminine characteristics was another sign of this tender devotion. The prayers of Anselm, according to Cabassut, may have been the source of the devotion to "Our Mother Christ," which enjoyed considerable popularity in the late Middle Ages,[111] when all the feminine aspects of Christian piety were emphasized. The cult of the Virgin was paralleled by the cults of other female saints which either began or became prominent in the twelfth century. Saxer has shown that the cult of Mary Magdalen was at its height in the twelfth century, then declined, but revived in the fifteenth century, thus forming a graph of liturgical and devotional interest parallel to the graph of popularity of twelfth-century spiritual texts.[112] The devotions of St. Anne and of the Conception of the Virgin started in the twelfth century, according to Wilmart, who also attributed to Anselm and Bernard the new importance attached to the episode of Mary and John (the most feminine of the apostles) at the foot of the cross.[113] Bernard's personal devotion to Mary has often been exaggerated, and he was certainly not primarily a Mariologist;[114] but he played an important part in the later development of Mariology, right down to the eighteenth century; and the miracle of the lactation, though of relatively late origin, expresses a spiritual truth in associating Cistercian piety with the maternal and feminine emphasis of later spirituality.[115]

These manifestations of emotionalism and sensuousness may not appeal to the more restrained religious sentiments of modern Christianity. The passionate embraces given by Rupert of Deutz to an image of Christ and the desire of Hugh of Lincoln to gather and drink the sweat of our Lord seem downright unattractive today.[116] They were authentic touches of twelfth-century spirituality, however, and were the physical counterpart of the emotional yearning which culminated centuries later in the erotic fantasies of the late medieval mystics and the melting ecstacy of Bernini's St. Theresa. Even the processions of penitential flagellants, who expressed the characteristic flamboyance of late medieval piety, can be traced to Dominic Loricatus and the practice of voluntary flagellation in twelfth-century monasteries. It was recognized as a public penance in the thirteenth century, continued in the fourteenth century in spite of official disapproval, and flourished particularly, in both orthodox and heretical circles, in the fifteenth century.[117]

Not all contemporaries approved of these elaborate displays, and efforts were made in the fourteenth and fifteenth centuries, as in the twelfth, to prune and purify the liturgy.[118] Ralph of Rivo, who was dean of Tongres from 1383 until 1403, has been called "the last representative of the old Roman liturgy;" he tried to draw a distinction between obligatory liturgical ceremonies and optional devotions.[119] Among other things, he revived the ancient theme of the Psalms as a biblical source-book on Christ.[120] More generally, the efforts to systematize the meditations on the life of Christ culminated for lay piety in the late medieval Books of Hours.[121]

The development of methodical meditation was one of the most important contributions of twelfth-century spirituality. Vernet called it "one of the great facts of the history of medieval spirituality"; and for Kirk "the discovery that worship need be none the worse and may be all the better for being orderly" was (together with the fact that "piety ceased to be the prerogative of the cloister") one of the "startling advances" of Christianity between the twelfth and sixteenth centuries.[122] The acme of this development was marked by the *Spiritual Exercises* of Ignatius Loyola,[123] and it is therefore fitting to conclude this paper with a consideration of the importance for Loyola of twelfth-century spirituality. Hugo Rahner said in his book, *The Spirituality of St. Ignatius Loyola,* that:

It is a well-known fact that the Spiritual Exercises have been subjected to research from every possible angle for the purpose of discovering real or pretended sources from which Inigo de Loyola is supposed to have drawn his teaching. . . . It has been supposed . . . that the chief source for the Ignatian streams of piety was to be found in the "modern devotion" (*devotio moderna*) of the fifteenth century. Successively, Cisneros, Erasmus of Rotterdam, Alonzo de Madrid, Gerard of Zütphen, John Maubernus [Mombaer], even Werner of Saint Blaise and Pseudo-Bernard, who flourished at the height of the Middle Ages, were rated as "indubitably" proven authorities for whole sections in the text of the Exercises. This course has led nowhere. What, in the end,

[47]

was the upshot of all these laborious inquiries? Nothing but the simple fact that Inigo read only these three books: *The Life of Christ* of Ludolph of Saxony, *The Golden Legend,* and *The Imitation of Christ.*[124]

Even through these works alone, however, and through the religious atmosphere in which he was raised, Loyola owed a heavy debt to medieval spirituality, and in particular to the twelfth century.[125]

This is shown simply in the title of his most famous work: "Spiritual exercises to conquer oneself and to order one's life without coming to a decision through any affection which is disordered."[126] The history of the expression *spiritualia exercitia* has been studied by several scholars. In the sense of physical asceticism, it occurs frequently in religious literature as far back as the fifth century;[127] but it was first applied to prayer and meditation in the twelfth century. Alexandre Brou in his book on *Ignatian Methods of Prayer* cited the contributions of Bernard, Aelred, William of St. Thierry, Guigo II, and the Victorines, to whom can be added Anselm, Guigo I, Bernard of Portes, and Adam of Dryburg. "The beginnings of methodical prayer are to be found in these contemplatives of the twelfth century," said Brou. "They are not satisfied with saying 'make your prayer'; they have pointed out how we should set about it, and what acts it would be good to make."[128] Guigo I of La Chartreuse used "spiritual exercises" in the same sense as Loyola;[129] and in the *Scala claustralium* of Guigo II, which was widely read in the late Middle Ages, Brou found the essential elements of the methods of prayer of Louis of Granada, Loyola, and Francis of Sales.[130] William of St. Thierry not only referred five times in his *Golden Letter* to "spiritual exercises," of the mind as well as of the body, but also used the expression *vitam ordinare,* which has been considered by one scholar the possible source of Loyola's reference in his title to ordering one's life. "Learn within your cell . . ." wrote William, "to be master of yourself, to order your life, to compose your habits, to judge yourself, to accuse yourself to yourself, and often to condemn and punish [yourself]."[131] Whether or

[48]

not Loyola actually read this passage (which is very doubtful),
he shared its view of the nature of the religious life.

A similar comparison can be made for the meditation on
the two standards, where Loyola saw Christ and the Devil as
two rival military leaders summoning men to their standards.
This meditation has been called "the germ of the Society of
Jesus,"[132] and its sources have been sought in both the Bible
and the works of the Fathers.[133] Most scholars are now agreed
that the specific form of the conflict as depicted by Loyola
derived from the account of Christ as king of Jerusalem and
the Devil as king of Babylon in the *Golden Legend*.[134] This
account in turn was based on Augustine, but it was also influenced by the twelfth-century spirituality of action and struggle. Hugh of St. Victor wrote in the prologue to his *De sacramentis,* for instance, that:

The Incarnate Word is our King, who came into this world to war
with the devil; and all the saints who were before His coming are
soldiers, as it were, going before their King, and those who have
come after and will come, even to the end of the world, are soldiers
following their King. And the King Himself is in the midst of
His army and proceeds protected and surrounded on all sides by
His columns. And although in a multitude as vast as this the
kind of arms differ in the sacraments and observance of the peoples
preceding and following, yet all are really serving the one king
and following the one banner; all are pursuing the one enemy
and are being crowned by the one victory.[135]

The similarity of this conception to that of Loyola is striking,
as is that of several later twelfth-century sources to which
various scholars have drawn attention.[136] They all, as Wolter
pointed out, reflect the spirituality of the Crusades, which developed in the twelfth century and influenced chivalric thought
throughout the Middle Ages.[137]

There is no need to search either in this passage or in the
other examples cited here for verbal similarities or direct influences of twelfth-century works on late medieval spirituality;
the similarities lie on a deeper level of religious needs and attitudes. The point being made here is that in religious history,

unlike intellectual history, the four centuries from the twelfth to the sixteenth must be seen as a whole and that the turning point in medieval religious history, as Wilmart and Chenu emphasized, falls in the late eleventh and twelfth centuries, when (in Wilmart's words) "the development of which the manifestations are clear in the fifteenth century began."[138] Though men's feelings about God and themselves continued to change in this period, they did not change out of recognition, and they never lost touch, direct or indirect, with the works of spirituality written in the twelfth century. Generation after generation of Christians found in these works a religious message adequate to their needs, a message the elements of which were later developed and elaborated but the essence of which remained unchanged.[139] A parallel development can be seen in the history of art, where the change of Christian vision in the twelfth century developed into the pathetic and extravagant realism of the late Middle Ages. The Isenheim alterpiece, however different at first sight, shows in its full bloom the emotional concentration on Christ's humanity and suffering of which the first signs appear in the art of the twelfth century.[140]

By isolating such individual themes, there is a danger of exaggerating the overall resemblances between the two ages. The religious writers and artists of the fifteenth and sixteenth centuries used traditional elements in new ways. They were concerned with different problems and reached different solutions than writers and artists in the twelfth century. But their religious needs and attitudes can be understood only in the context of a spirituality going back to the prescholastic period and cutting across the national distinctions and theological differences of the late Middle Ages. These feelings, in turn, help to explain the successes and failures of the religious movements of this confused age. They do not tell the whole story, but the story they tell is different from the usual account of the Reformation and Counter-Reformation and one of which the beginnings are deeply buried in the religious history of the Middle Ages.

Postscript

My lecture is printed here substantially as it was delivered in Chapel Hill, but I should like to amplify three points which were raised in subsequent discussion.

(1) Some listeners suggested that I gave too much credit for a humane view of marriage to the notorious misogynist Bernard of Clairvaux. Bernard certainly esteemed the life of a married layman far less highly than that of a celibate monk, and he used marriage metaphors to describe spiritual rather than physical relationships. His very use of such metaphors, however, implied that the human state of marriage was not entirely without a relative worth and dignity of its own. The dangers of dualism, furthermore, of which Bernard was aware from contemporary heresies, promoted a more positive view of human marriage. Hugh of Amiens, for instance, in his treatise against the heretics and in his commentary on the Hexaemeron, specifically praised the value, justice, and sanctity of marriage and stressed that Jesus Himself was born "not from a simple virgin but from a married woman": *Contra haereticos*, III, 4 (*Patrologia latina*, CXCII, 1289 AB) and F. Lecomte, "Un commentaire scripturaire du XIIe siècle: Le 'Tractatus in Hexaemeron' de Hugues d'Amiens (Archévêque de Rouen 1130–1164)," *Archives d'histoire doctrinale et littéraire du Moyen Age*, XXV (1958), 278. This valuation of marriage is not very high, but it suggests an important change of attitude even among monks like Bernard.

(2) Many twelfth-century spiritual works may have been known in the late Middle Ages through *florilegia* and collections of excerpts, which were extensively used in the composition of sermons and other literary genres. The number of manuscripts and early printed editions, however, suggests that many of these works were read in their entirety, and the inclusion of selected passages in *florilegia* shows in itself their appeal to late medieval religious sentiments.

(3) Of the more serious charge of neglecting the thirteenth century, I may be guilty, but cite as extenuating circum-

stances that the importance of the thirteenth century has in the past, if anything, been overemphasized and that one of the purposes of my lecture was to argue that in the history of spirituality the thirteenth century was less important than the twelfth. This is not to deny that influential and widely read spiritual writers worked in the thirteenth century or that the scholastic theologians participated in the religious sentiments of their day. It is to suggest, rather, that their contribution to spirituality was less profound and original than in the areas of theology and philosophy. This is shown, for instance, by the number of spiritual works, both earlier and later, which went under the name of Bonaventura and by the fact that a figure such as Groote almost entirely neglected the thirteenth century (as I have done) and was influenced primarily by works written in the twelfth century: see R. R. Post, *The Modern Devotion Confrontation with Reformation and Humanism* (Studies in Medieval and Reformation Thought, 3; Leiden, 1968), pp. 317, which unfortunately came into my hands too late for use elsewhere in this paper.

NOTES

1. Lucien Febvre, "Une question mal posée: Les origines de la réforme française et le problème des causes de la réforme" (1929), reprinted in *Au coeur religieux du XVIe siècle* (Paris, 1957), pp. 3–70.

2. *Ibid.*, p. 26.

3. *Ibid.*, p. 69.

4. Cf. Alain Dufour, "Humanisme et Réformation: État de la question," in *Histoire politique et psychologie historique* (Geneva, 1966), pp. 42–43, who suggests that one result of the historical application of existentialism has been to isolate reformers from their historical context.

5. William James, *The Varieties of Religious Experience* (New York, 1902), p. 108.

6. *Ibid.*, p. 325.

7. Cf. *ibid.*, p. 109.

8. Iris Origo, *The World of San Bernardino* (New York, 1962), pp. 252–53.

9. Gerhart B. Ladner, "*Homo Viator:* Mediaeval Ideas on Alienation and Order," *Speculum*, XLII (1967), 255.

10. George Rosen, *Madness in Society* (Chicago, 1968), pp. 199 and 224, who also stressed (p. 7) that the witch hunts were complex phenomena involving political, social, psychological, and ideological factors.

11. Ladner, "*Homo Viator*," pp. 256–58.

12. Jean Gerson, *Oeuvres complètes*, ed. P. Glorieux (Paris, 1960–), III, 249; cf. *De mystica theologia*, ed. A. Combes (Thesaurus mundi, 9; Lugano, 1958), pp. 50–51, and André Combes, *La théologie mystique de Gerson: Profil de son évolution* (Spiritualitas, 1–2; Rome, 1963–64), II, 244.

13. Cited by Hanna Gray, "Valla's *Encomium* of *St. Thomas Aquinas* and the Humanist Conception of Christian Antiquity," *Essays in History and Literature Presented . . . to Stanley Pargellis* (Chicago, 1965), p. 48.

14. P. O. Kristeller, "Giovanni Pico della Mirandola and his Sources," *L'opera e il pensiero di Giovanni Pico della Mirandola nella storia dell'umanesimo* (Florence, 1965), I, 80.

15. P. O. Kristeller, *Renaissance Philosophy and the Mediaeval Tradition* (Wimmer Lecture, 15; Latrobe, 1966), p. 38.

16. Herbert Grundmann, "Neue Beiträge zur Geschichte der religiösen Bewegungen im Mittelalter" (1955), reprinted in *Religiöse Bewegungen im Mittelalter*, 2nd ed. (Hildesheim, 1961), pp. 531 and 537.

17. Cf. J. A. Jungmann, "Die Abwehr des germanischen Arianismus und der Umbruck der religiösen Kultur im frühen Mittelalter," *Zeitschrift für katholische Theologie*, LXIX (1947), 36–99.

18. André Wilmart, *Auteurs spirituels et textes dévots du moyen âge latin* (Paris, 1932), p. 59.

19. *Ibid.*, p. 63: cf. also pp. 505–6.

20. Richard Southern, *The Making of the Middle Ages* (New Haven, 1953), pp. 227, 228, 232; cf. M.-D. Chenu, *La théologie au douzième siècle* (Études de philosophie médiévale, 45; Paris, 1957), pp. 9, 223–24, 239; Robert Javelet, *Image et ressemblance au douzième siècle de saint Anselme à Alain de Lille* (Strasbourg, 1967), I, 455.

21. E. Ph. Goldschmidt, *Medieval Texts and their First Appearance in Print* (Supplement to the Bibliographical Society's Transactions, 16; London, 1943), p. 51.

22. Leopold Janauschek, *Bibliographia Bernardina* (Xenia Bernardina, 4; Vienna, 1891), pp. 3–133.

23. Henri Bremond, *Histoire littéraire du sentiment religieux en France* (Paris, 1915–32), III, 26.

24. Marcel Viller, "Le *Speculum monachorum* et la 'Dévotion moderne,'" *Revue d'ascétique et de mystique*, III (1922), 45–56; Wilmart, *Auteurs spirituels*, pp. 230–31; and other references in my article on "The Popularity of Twelfth Century Spiritual Writers in the Late Middle Ages," *Renaissance Studies in Honor of Hans Baron* (Florence, 1971), pp. 5–28.

25. Cf. Kristeller, *Renaissance Philosophy*, p. 11.

26. Augustin Renaudet, *Préréforme et humanisme à Paris pendant les premières guerres d'Italie (1494–1517)* (Bibliothèque de l'Institut français de Florence, I, 6; Paris, 1916), pp. 73, 113.

27. Combes, *Théologie mystique*, II, 53–54; cf. I, 63, 103; II, 566.

28. *Ibid.*, I, 159–60; II, 97, 140–43. Gerson was also indebted to Bernard for his doctrines of "industria," "defectio," and "reparatio' (I, 121; II, 124–36).

29. Roger Baron, "L'influence de Hugues de Saint-Victor," *Recherches de théologie ancienne et médiévale*, XXII (1955), 71.

30. *Deonise Hid Diuinite*, ed. Phyllis Hodgson (Early English Text Society, 231; London, 1955), p. xxxv.

31. Robert Javelet, "Thomas Gallus et Richard de Saint-Victor mystiques," *Recherches de théologie ancienne et médiévale*, XXIX (1962), 206.

32. Edmond Vansteenberghe, *Le cardinal Nicolas de Cues (1401–1464): L'action—la pensée* (Lille, 1920), pp. 42, 423–24, 431; Raymond Klibansky, *The Continuity of the Platonic Tradition* (London [1950]), pp. 28, 35–36.

33. Gray, "Valla's *Encomium of St. Thomas Aquinas*," p. 43.

34. Kristeller, *Renaissance Philosophy*, pp. 37–38; Gray, "Valla's *Encomium of St. Thomas Aquinas*," p. 43.

35. Theodor Mommsen, "Petrarch's Conception of the 'Dark Ages'" (1942), reprinted in *Medieval and Renaissance Studies*, ed. Eugene Rice (Ithaca, 1959), p. 129.

36. Pierre de Nolhac, *Pétrarche et l'humanisme* (Bibliothèque littéraire de la Renaissance, N.S. 1–2; Paris, 1907), I, 104, 113; II, 207–8, 216–25.

37. P. O. Kristeller, "Augustine and the Early Renaissance," *Review of Religion*, IX (1944), 346; cf. also his *Renaissance Thought* (New York, 1961), p. 78.

38. Cf. Eleanor Rathbone, "Master Alberic of London, *Mythographus tertius vaticanus*," *Medieval and Renaissance Studies*, I.1 (1941), 35–38; and Elisabeth Pellegrin, "Un manuscrit des 'Derivationes' d'Osbern de Gloucester annoté par Pétrarche," *Italia medioevale e umanistica*, III (1960), 263–66.

39. P. O. Kristeller, "Pier Candido Decembrio and his Unpublished Treatise on the Immortality of the Soul," *The Classical Tradition: Literary and Historical Studies in Honor of Harry Caplan* (Ithaca, 1966), pp. 536–58.

40. Eugene Rice, "The Humanist Idea of Christian Antiquity: Lefèvre d'Étaples and his Circle," *Studies in the Renaissance*, IX (1962), 141.

41. See the lists in Renaudet, *Préréforme;* and Goldschmidt, *Medieval Texts.* The first edition of Peter the Venerable was published at Paris in 1522.

42. Renaudet, *Préréforme*, p. 521 (cf. pp. 495, 597, 599–600, 601–2, 623, 625–26, 635–37), and Goldschmidt, *Medieval Texts*, pp. 52–57.

43. F. 22ᵛ or the 1508 Paris edition of Bernard's works; cf. Renaudet, *Préréforme*, p. 500; Goldschmidt, *Medieval Texts*, p. 124; and (on Clichtove's edition of Hugh of St. Victor) Roger Baron, *Science et sagesse chez Hugues de Saint-Victor* (Paris, 1957), p. 234.

44. On the material in this paragraph, see Odon Lottin, *Psychologie et*

morale aux XIIe et XIIIe siècles (Louvain-Gembloux, 1942–1960), II, 421–65, and IV, 309–486.

45. Cf. Bernard, *De gratia et libero arbitrio*, II, 4 (ed. Jean Leclercq [Rome, 1957–] III, 168–69); and John of Salisbury, *Policraticus*, VII, 25 (ed. C. C. J. Webb [Oxford, 1909], II, 217).

46. Lottin, *Psychologie*, I, 222; cf. Roger Baron, "L'idée de liberté chez S. Anselme et Hugues de Saint–Victor," *Recherches de théologie ancienne et médiévale*, XXXII (1965), 117–21.

47. Cf. M.-A. Dimier, "Pour la fiche *Spiritus libertatis*," *Revue du moyen âge latin*, III (1947), 56–60; Herbert Grundmann, "Freiheit als religiöses, politisches und persönliches Postulat im Mittelalter," *Historische Zeitschrift*, CLXXXIII (1957), 23–53, esp. 45–47; and (on the late Middle Ages) Romana Guarnieri, in *Dictionnaire de spiritualité*, V (Paris, 1962–64), 1241–68.

48. Adam of Perseigne, *Lettres*, ed. Jean Bouvet, I (Sources chrétiennes, 66; Paris, 1960), p. 122. Bernard's triple distinction of liberty comes in *De gratia et libero arbitrio*, III, 7 (ed. Leclercq, III, 171).

49. Southern, *Making of the Middle Ages*, p. 227.

50. Ermenegildo Bertola, "Il socratismo cristiano nel XII secolo," *Rivista di filosofia neo-scolastica*, LI (1959), 262–64; Javelet, *Image*, I, 205–6, 368–71.

51. Javelet, *Image*, I, 181–82, 197, 247.

52. Richard of St. Victor, *Benjamin major*, III, 13 (*Patrologia latina*, CXCVI, 123 A). The precision and elegance of the Latin is lost in the translation. Cf. the view of Bernard in his sermon *De diversis*, 12, 2 (Gaume ed. [Paris, 1839], I.2, 2339 A).

53. Cf. Javelet, *Image*, I, 297, 454–57.

54. On this saying, which is found in various forms in a number of twelfth-century texts, see the references in *The Letters of Peter the Venerable*, ed. Giles Constable (Harvard Historical Studies, 78; Cambridge, Mass., 1967), I, 60, n. 2.

55. James, *Varieties of Religious Experience*, pp. 80, 361.

56. Caesarius of Heisterbach, *Dialogus miraculorum*, X, 6 (ed. J. Strange [Cologne, 1851] II, 221–22). This is the earliest example of such an attitude cited by Oechslin in his article on "Dépouillement" in the *Dictionnaire de spiritualité*, III (Paris, 1954–57), 472.

57. Jean Gerson, *Opera omnia* (Antwerp, 1706), III, 1125.

58. Cf. the confessions of the mid-fourteenth century heretic John of Brünn, in W. Wattenbach, "Über die Secte der Brüder vom freien Geiste," *Sitzungsberichte der königlich preussichen Akademie der Wissenschaften zu Berlin*, 1887 (No. 29), pp. 529–31.

59. Bernard, Sermon *In Annunc.*, I, 1–3 (Gaume ed., I.2, 2093–95).

60. *Patrologia latina*, CLXXXIV, 554 AB; cf. Javelet, *Image*, II, 99: "Son texte comme ceux d'Isaac est à considérer dans une étude des lointains préliminaires de la théorie de Luther sur la prédestination et la justification." On this treatise, which closely follows Bernard's ideas, and on two other similar treatises, see P. Delhaye, "Dans le sillage de S. Bernard: Trois petits traités *De conscientia*," *Cîteaux in de Nederlanden*, V (1954), 92–103.

61. Bernard, Sermon *In Annunc.* I, 4 (Gaume ed., I.2 2095 B).

62. James, *Varieties of Religious Experience*, pp. 109–10 and 246–48.

63. Cf. Carl Stange, *Bernhard von Clairvaux* (Studien der Luther-Akademie, N.F. 3; Berlin, 1954), p. 5.

64. Cf. Heinrich Boehmer, *Luther and the Reformation in the Light of Modern Research*, tr. E. S. G. Potter (New York, 1930), p. 70; Ernst Benz, "Luther und Bernhard von Clairvaux," *Eckart*, XXIII (1953), 62; and Roland

Mousnier, "Saint Bernard et Luther," *Saint Bernard: Homme d'Église* (Témoignages: Cahiers de La Pierre-qui-Vire, 38–39; Paris, 1953), p. 152.

65. Stange, *Bernhard*, p. 8.

66. Weimar ed., *Tischreden*, IV, 480, No. 4772.

67. *Ibid.*, LVIII.1, 178–80, citing Luther's references to Bernard.

68. *Ibid.*, VIII, 601.

69. Heinrich Denifle, *Luther und Luthertum in der ersten Entwickelung*, 2nd ed. (Mainz, 1904–9), I, 40–49 (showing that the passage was not a deathbed confession but taken from the sermon *Super Cantica*, 20, 1 [ed. Leclercq, I, 114]), whose views are repeated by Hartmann Grisar, *Luther*, tr. E. M. Lamond, ed. Luigi Cappadelta (London, 1913–17), I, 18, 88, 181, and IV, 88–89.

70. Cf. Boehmer, *Luther*, pp. 70–71; Stange, *Bernhard*, p. 5; Mousnier, "Saint Bernard et Luther," pp. 155–56, who also discussed (pp. 159–65) some of the differences between the theologies of Bernard and Luther. C. C. J. Webb, *Studies in the History of Natural Philosophy* (Oxford, 1915), p. 231, suggested that Luther's dislike of reason and rationalism was the reason for his liking Bernard.

71. Mousnier, "Saint Bernard et Luther," pp. 165–69.

72. Cf. Benz, "Luther und Bernhard," pp. 61-62.

73. Henri Strohl, *L'épanouissement de la pensée religieuse de Luther de 1515 à 1520* (Études d'histoire et de philosophie religieuses publiées par la Faculté de théologie protestante de l'Université de Strasbourg, 9; Strasbourg-Paris, 1924), pp. 113–44; cf. Benz, "Luther und Bernhard," p. 64, and Mousnier, "Saint Bernard et Luther," p. 166. Lewis Spitz, "Current Accents in Luther Study: 1960–67," *Theological Studies*, XXVIII (1967), 554, comments on the lack of recent work on Luther's relation to mysticism and his knowledge of pre-scholastic writers.

74. Strohl, *Épanouissement*, p. 143.

75. Weimar, ed., VII, 632, and XXIII, 415.

76. G. Morin, "Un critique en liturgie au XIIe siècle: Le traité inédit d'Hervé de Bourgdieu *De correctione quorumdam lectionum*," *Revue bénédictine*, XXIV (1907), 43; cf. Klaus Schreiner, "Zum Wahrheitsverständnis im Heiligen- und Reliquienwesen des Mittelalters," *Saeculum*, XVII (1966), 143, n. 61; and G. Ladner, in *Reallexikon für Antike und Christentum*, VI (Stuttgart, 1964–66), 265–66.

77. Giovanni Miccoli, *"Ecclesiae primitivae forma"* (1960), reprinted and expanded in *Chiesa gregoriana* (Storici antichi e moderni, N.S. 17; Florence, 1966), pp. 225–99, esp. 225–26.

78. Gordon Leff, "The Apostolic Ideal in Later Medieval Ecclesiology," *Journal of Theological Studies*, N.S., XVIII (1967), 58–82. Leff exaggerated somewhat in calling the ideal of the apostolic church "the great new ecclesiological fact of the later Middle Ages" (p. 71).

79. Roland Bainton, "Changing Ideas and Ideals in the Sixteenth Century" (1936), reprinted in his *Collected Papers in Church History*, I: *Early and Medieval Christianity* (Boston, 1962), p. 166.

80. G. R. Owst, *Literature and Pulpit in Medieval England*, 2nd ed. (Oxford-New York, 1961), p. 278.

81. John A. Junck, "Economic Conservatism, Papal Finance, and the Medieval Satires on Rome" (1961), reprinted in *Change in Medieval Society*, ed. Sylvia Thrupp (New York, 1964), p. 76.

82. E. R. Curtius, *European Literature and the Latin Middle Ages*, tr. W. R. Trask (New York, 1963), p. 124.

83. Cf. Robert Javelet, "Psychologie des auteurs spirituels du XIIe siècle," *Revue des sciences religieuses*, XXXIII (1959), 38.

84. *Dictionnaire d'histoire et de géographie ecclésiastiques*, XII (Paris, 1953), 394. On Aquinas, see Jean Leclercq, "La vie contemplative dans S. Thomas et dans la tradition," *Recherches de théologie ancienne et médiévale*, XXVIII (1961), 251–68.

85. Gerhoh of Reichersberg, *Opusculum de aedificio Dei*, c. 28 (*Patrologia latina*, CXCIV, 1267 C).

86. Philip of Harvengt, *De institutione clericorum*, IV, 99 (*Patrologia latina*, CCIII, 802 AB).

87. Peter the Venerable, Ep. 58 (ed. Constable, I, 187–88).

88. Cf. Ivo of Chartres, Ep. 245 (*Patrologia latina*, CLXII, 251–52). On marriage doctrine in the twelfth century, see Gabriel Le Bras, "Le mariage dans la théologie et le droit de l'Église du XIe au XIIIe siècle," *Cahiers de civilization médiévale*, XI (1968) 191–202; and the two articles by James Brundage, "The Crusader's Wife: A Canonistic Quandary" and "The Crusader's Wife Revisited" in *Studia Gratiana*, XII (1967), 425–42 and XIV (1967), 241–52. On the equality of men and women in twelfth-century theology, see Javelet, *Image*, I, 236–45.

89. Sermon 83 *Super Cantica*, II, 5 (ed. Leclercq, II, 301).

90. Isaac of L'Étoile, Sermon XL (*Patrologia latina*, CXCIV, 1824 B).

91. Yvonne Labande-Mailfert, "L'iconographie des laïcs dans la société religieuse aux XIe et XIIe siècles," *I laici nella "Societas christiana" dei secoli XI e XII* (Pubblicazioni dell'Università cattolica del Sacro Cuore: Contributi, 3rd S.: Miscellanea del Centro di Studi medioevali, 5; Milan, 1968), p. 513 and pl. IX, fig. 26, who remarks that, "C'est une oeuvre unique dans l'art roman pour l'expression de l'amour conjugal."

92. Hans Baron, "Secularization of Wisdom and Political Humanism in the Renaissance: Rice's *Renaissance Idea of Wisdom*," *Journal of the History of Ideas*, XXI (1960), 137.

93. Hans Baron, "Cicero and the Roman Civic Spirit in the Middle Ages and the Early Renaissance" (1938), reprinted and revised in *Lordship and Community in Medieval Europe*, ed. Fredric Cheyette (New York, 1968), pp. 291–314, who shows that the beginnings of the change are found in Italy in the twelfth century.

94. *Dialecticae disputationes*, I, 8 (*Opera omnia* [Basel, 1540, reprinted Turin, 1962] I, 660); and *De professione religiosorum* (ed. M. J. Vahlen, reprinted *ibid.*, II, 287–325); cf. Gray, "Valla's *Encomium of St. Thomas Aquinas*," p. 50.

95. Émile Telle, *Érasme de Rotterdam et le septième sacrement* (Geneva, 1954), p. 6.

96. Combes, *Théologie mystique*, I, 382, cf. I, 159–60.

97. Heiko Oberman, "Gabriel Biel and Late Medieval Mysticism," *Church History*, XXX (1961), 269.

98. Paul Wilpert, "Vita Contemplativa und Vita Activa: Eine Kontroverse des 15. Jahrhunderts," *Passauer Studien: Festschrift für Bischof Dr. Dr. Simon Konrad Landersdorfer* (Passau, 1953), p. 226.

99. Gray, "Valla's *Encomium of St. Thomas Aquinas*," p. 50.

100. Cf. Bernard, *De gratia et libero arbitrio*, II, 4 (ed. Leclercq, III, 168–69); *Sermo in feria IV hebdomadae sanctae*, 12 (Gaume ed., I.3, 1945–46); *Sermo in festo omnium sanctorum*, I, 8 (*ibid.*, 2190); etc.

101. Bernard, Ep. 250.4 (Gaume ed., I.1, 525 A).

102. Bernhard Lohse, *Mönchtum und Reformation: Luthers Auseinander-*

setzung mit dem Mönchsideal des Mittelalters (Göttingen, 1963), pp. 201–379, esp. 377–79.

103. Cf. Georg Schreiber, "Monasterium und Frömmigkeit," *Zeitschrift für Aszese und Mystik*, XVI (1941), 19–31 (of which I have seen only the analysis in the *Revue d'histoire ecclésiastique*, XXXVIII [1942] 230), who stressed the influence of twelfth-century monastic spirituality on later devotions.

104. R. W. Southern, *Saint Anselm and his Biographer* (Birkbeck Lectures, 1959; Cambridge, 1963), pp. 47 and 350, cf. pp. 37–38 on the continued popularity of Anselm's prayers; and Wilmart, *Auteurs spirituels*, pp. 506–7.

105. Southern, *Making of the Middle Ages*, p. 232.

106. Josef Stadlhuber, "Das Laienstundengebet vom Leiden Christi in seinem mittelalterlichen Fortleben," *Zeitschrift für katholische Theologie*, LXXII (1950), 289–91.

107. F. Baix and C. Lambot, *La dévotion à l'Eucharistie et le VIIe centenaire de la Fête-Dieu* (Gembloux-Namur [1946]) pp. 22–26; cf. Edouard Dumoutet, *Le Christ selon la Chair et la vie liturgique au Moyen-Âge* (Paris, 1932), p. 147; Georg Schreiber, "Mittelalterliche Passionsmystik und Frömmigkeit: Der älteste Herz-Jesu-Hymnus," *Theologische Quartalschrift*, CXXII (1941), 41; and Gerhard Matern, *Zur Vorgeschichte und Geschichte der Fronleichnamsfeier besonders in Spanien* (Spanische Forschungen der Görresgesellschaft, II, 10; Münster, 1962), pp. 10–11.

108. Cf. Matern, *Fronleichnamsfeier*, pp. 17–33.

109. Wilmart, *Auteurs spirituels*, p. 583; cf. Stadlhuber, "Das Laienstundengebet," p. 309, on twelfth-century prayers to the Holy Wounds.

110. Georg Schreiber, "Prämonstratensische Frömmigkeit und die Anfänge des Herz-Jesu-Gedankens," *Zeitschrift für katholische Theologie*, LXIV (1940), 195–201, and his "Mittelalterliche Passionsmystik," pp. 32–44.

111. André Cabassut, "Une dévotion médiévale peu connue: La dévotion à *Jésus notre mère*," *Revue d'ascétique et de mystique*, XXV.2–4 (*Mélanges Marcel Viller*) (Toulouse, 1949), pp. 234–45.

112. Victor Saxer, *Le culte de Marie Madeleine en occident des origines à la fin du moyen âge* (Cahiers d'archéologie et d'histoire, 3; Auxerre-Paris, 1959), p. 355.

113. Wilmart, *Auteurs spirituels*, pp. 46–49 and 507.

114. H. Barré, "Saint Bernard, Docteur Marial," *Saint Bernard théologien* (Analecta sacri ordinis Cisterciensis, IX.3–4; Rome, 1953), pp. 92–113.

115. See several articles on Bernard's influence on Spanish Mariology in *Estudios marianos*, XIV (1954); and on the legend of the lactation, Léon Dewez and Albert van Iterson, "La lactation de saint Bernard: Legende et iconographie," *Cîteaux in de Nederlanden*, VII (1956), 165–89.

116. Rupert of Deutz, *Commentarium in Matthaeum*, 12 (*Patrologia latina*, CLXVIII, 1590); *Magna vita sancti Hugonis*, ed. Decima Douie and Hugh Farmer (Medieval Texts; Edinburgh, 1961–62), II, 14–15.

117. Cf. Paul Bailly, in *Dictionnaire de spiritualité*, V, 392–400.

118. Cf. Paul Lejay, "Les accroissements de l'office quotidien," *Revue du clergé français*, XL (1904), 139–40.

119. Cunibert Mohlberg, *Radulph de Rivo: Der letzte Vertreter der altrömischen Liturgie* (Université de Louvain: Recueil de travaux publiés par les membres des conférences d'histoire et de philologie, 29, 42; Louvain-Paris-Münster, 1911–15), *passim* (for twelfth-century writers used by Ralph, see index s.n. Arnulf of Bohéries, Bernard, Honorius, Hugh, Rupert) and Lejay, "Les accroissements," pp. 139–40.

120. Balthasar Fischer, "Le Christ dans les psaumes," *La Maison-Dieu*,

XXVII (1951), 108, n. 84, and Pierre Salmon, *Les "Tituli psalmorum" des manuscrits latins* (Paris, 1959), p. 35.

121. Stadlhuber, "Das Laienstundengebet," pp. 282–91.

122. Félix Vernet, *La spiritualité médiévale* (Bibliothèque catholique des sciences religieuses, 33; Paris, 1929), p. 125; Kenneth E. Kirk, *The Vision of God: The Christian Doctrine of the Summum Bonum*, 2nd ed. (Bampton Lectures, 1928; London, 1932), p. 412; cf. M. Bulteel, "Bijdrage tot de Studie van het Beschouwend Gebed in de Twaalfde Eewe" (unpublished thesis, Louvain, 1952), cited by Maurice Laporte, *Aux sources de la vie cartusienne* (La Chartreuse, 1960), II, 526, saying that Bulteel stresses "l'importance du 12ème siècle dans la naissance de la méditation comme exercise."

123. Cf. Kirk, *Vision*, p. 401 ("He [Ignatius] is in the true line of succession from S. Paul, S. Bernard and S. Francis."); David Knowles, *From Pachomius to Ignatius: A Study in the Constitutional History of the Religious Orders* (Sarum Lectures, 1964–65; Oxford, 1966), pp. 88–94.

124. Hugo Rahner, *The Spirituality of St. Ignatius Loyola*, tr. Francis Smith (Westminster, Md., 1953), pp. 23–24; cf. Léonce de Grandmaison, "Les *Exercises* de Saint Ignace dans l'édition des *Monumenta*," *Recherches de science religieuse*, X (1920), 396; Joseph de Guibert, *The Jesuits: Their Spiritual Doctrine and Practice*, tr. William Young, ed. George Ganss (Chicago, 1964), pp. 153–57; and, for a bibliography on the subject of the sources of the *Exercises*, Jean-François Gilmont and Paul Daman, *Bibliographie Ignatienne (1894–1957)* (Museum Lessianum: Section historique, 17; Paris-Louvain [1958]), Nos. 1198–1224.

125. On Ludolph's *Life of Christ*, see François Vandenbroucke, in Jean Leclercq, François Vandenbroucke, and Louis Bouyer, *La spiritualité du moyen âge* (Paris, 1961), p. 547 (calling Ludolph "assez peu original"). The debt of *The Imitation of Christ* to twelfth-century writers, especially Bernard, Hugh, and Richard, is generally acknowledged: cf. E. F. Jacob, *Essays in the Conciliar Epoch*, 2nd ed. (Manchester, 1953), pp. 139–53.

126. De Guibert, *Jesuits*, p. 111.

127. See L. Hertling, "De usu nominis exercitiorum spiritualium ante S. P. Ignatium," *Archivum historicum Societatis Iesu*, II (1933), 316–18; and Heinrich Bacht, "Die frühmonastischen Grundlagen ignatianischer Frömmigkeit: Zu einigen Grundbegriffen der Exerzitien," *Ignatius von Loyola*, ed. Friedrich Wulf (Würzburg, 1956), p. 231.

128. Alexandre Brou, *Ignatian Methods of Prayer*, tr. William Young (Milwaukee, 1949), p. 6; cf. Marcel Viller's review of the second volume of Pourrat's *Spiritualité chrétienne* in the *Revue d'ascétique et de mystique*, III (1922), 78–79; and Laporte, *Sources*, II, 525–27, and VI, 541–43; and Pedro de Leturia, "Lecturas ascéticas y lecturas místicas entre los Jesuítas del siglo XVI," *Archivio italiano per la storia della pietà*, II (1959), 3–4.

129. A. de Meyer and J. M. de Smet, *Guigo's "Consuetudines" van de eerste Kartuizers* (Mededelingen van de koninklijke vlaamse Academie voor Wetenschappen, Letteren en schone Kunsten van België: Klasse der Letteren, XIII.6; Brussels, 1951), p. 53, n. 1; Laporte, *Sources*, II, 525–27 (cf. also VI, 541–43).

130. Brou, *Ignatian Prayer*, pp. 5–6.

131. H. Pinard de la Boullaye, "Aux sources des Exercises: Guillaume de Saint-Thierry et Vincent Ferrer," *Revue d'ascétique et de mystique*, XXVI (1950), 327–46. Vincent Ferrer certainly used the *Golden Letter*, but Pinard de la Boullaye considers it more likely that Loyola used it directly rather than through Ferrer.

132. C. A. Kneller, "Zu den Kontroversen über den hl. Ignatius von Loyola,

II: Quellen der Exerzitien?" *Zeitschrift für katholische Theologie,* XLIX (1925), 164. The importance of this meditation was repeatedly emphasized by Rahner, *Spirituality,* pp. xii, 22, 36, 56, 105, but De Guibert, *Jesuits,* pp. 172–74, tried to play down the military character of Ignatian spirituality; cf. also Hans Wolter, "Elemente der Kreuzzugsfrömmigkeit in der Spiritualität des heiligen Ignatius," *Ignatius von Loyola,* ed. Friedrich Wulf (Würzburg, 1956), pp. 113–50.

133. Cf. Ferdinand Tournier, "Les *deux cités* dans la littérature chrétienne," *Études,* CXXIII (1910), 644–65; Kneller, "Zu den Kontroversen," p. 113; and Bacht, "Die frühmonastischen," in *Ignatius,* pp. 249–50, who calls the first part of Evagrius's *De diversis malignis cogitationibus* a commentary on the meditation on the two standards. For further references, see Gilmont and Daman, *Bibliographie,* Nos. 1635–50.

134. This was first suggested, I believe, by Kneller, "Zu den Kontroversen," p. 164, and was accepted by Rahner, *Spirituality,* p. 28, and others.

135. Hugh of St. Victor, *De sacramentis,* tr. Roy J. Deferrari (Mediaeval Academy of America Publication 58; Cambridge, 1951), pp. 2–3; cf. Javelet, *Image,* I, 334 and 457, who considered this passage a prefiguration of Ignatius's meditation. On the possible influence of Hugh's mysticism on Loyola, see Baron "Influence de Hugues," p. 69.

136. See Tournier, "Les *deux cités,*" pp. 648–53 and 658–62, where the texts of Augustine, Werner of St. Blaise, and Ignatius are cited in parallel columns. Though most scholars have not accepted Tournier's conclusions, De Guibert, *Jesuits,* p. 118, admitted that the resemblances between Werner and Loyola "are such that it is difficult to take them as a matter of chance and to refuse to admit some dependence in the present text of the *Exercises.*"

137. Wolter, "Elemente der Kreuzzugsfrömmigkeit," pp. 113–50, who mentions among other parallel themes the emphasis on the will of God, on Christ, *imitatio, vita apostolica,* the kingdom of Christ, *militia Christi,* forgiveness, consciousness of community, service, hospitality, poverty, and *gloria Dei.*

138. Wilmart, *Auteurs spirituels,* p. 506; and Chenu, *Théologie,* pp. 223–24 and 239. Gilson in his introduction to Chenu (p. 9) stated his view that the *devotio moderna* continued a current of spirituality going back to the twelfth century.

139. Jesuit novices in the sixteenth century were encouraged to read twelfth-century works but forbidden to read indiscriminately the works of late medieval mystical writers: see De Guibert, *Jesuits,* p. 218; and De Leturia, "Lecturas ascéticas," pp. 47–48. Among recommended works was Peter the Venerable's *De miraculis,* of which the G. G. Coulton (commenting on the edition printed at Douai in 1595) said, "We have here, therefore, a book which both twelfth-century and sixteenth-century monasticism recognized as typical and authoritative": *Life in the middle Ages* (Cambridge, 1935), IV, 110.

140. Louis Réau, *L'iconographie de l'art chrétien* (Paris, 1955–), II, 476–511; and Paul Thoby, *Le crucifix des origines au Concile de Trente* ([Nantes], 1959), *passim.* More generally, see Étienne Sabbe, "Le culte marial et la genèse de la sculpture médiévale," *Revue belge d'archéologie et d'histoire de l'art,* XX (1951), 101–25; and Southern, *Making of the Middle Ages,* pp. 237–40.

III

On Editing Shakespeare:
Annus Mirabilis

George Walton Williams
Duke University

In 1966, Professor Arthur Brown of University College, London, addressed this group on the topic "The Transmission of the Text"; but Professor Brown, before he was well into his paper, was tempted to change his title to "The Text—Does It Exist?"[1] I might then have addressed you on the topic "The Text—Does It Exist? Part II," or "The Text—Does It Exist Yet?" But we might all have become restive before that question was answered, and I therefore decided to address you on the process rather than on the thing itself.

I have taken the title of my paper from Professor Fredson Bowers' monograph, *On Editing Shakespeare and the Elizabethan Dramatists,*[2] assuming that such petty larceny is not denied to one of the sons of Fred; and I must ask you to assume in addition that the Text *Does* Exist, that it has endured Transmission, and that Editing Shakespeare is an activity of mankind which will always be with us, and which is rational and on the whole harmless. (The textual critic shares that characteristic with Dr. Johnson's lexicographer.) I say "always be with us" because the Utopia in which the perfect Shakespearian text exists is not yet, and further, is not likely to come in the day this Institute closes. The world of textual criticism still groaneth and travailleth together toward perfection.

We might begin our examination of the editing of Shakespeare's texts *ab ovo,* i.e., with a close study of the manuscripts

[61]

of Shakespeare's plays; but, as you well know, these documents are as numerous as the snakes in Ireland. Disappointed in that inquiry, we might then turn to the earliest printed forms of Shakespeare's plays and trace them to the first development of printing from movable types. We would not, happily, as Professor White demonstrated in his recent lecture, have to voyage to Korea in the 1390's—*ex oriente non lux*—but we might begin with the unknown Dutch printer in Haarlem who first used movable types in the West and whose printed books are alive at this day to testify it. And we might then, if we followed the Dutch legend, believe that Gutenberg stole the Hollander's mystery on Christmas Eve while the inventor was at Mass and spirited it off by a process known as stimulus diffusion to Mainz where he invented it again several years later.[3] Or we might, being more scholarly, believe that Gutenberg knew nothing of the Hollander's work and independently, after many years of highly sophisticated experiment in die-cutting, metallurgy, and carpentry, perfected the mystery of carving, casting, and pressing types.[4] We would recall that Gutenberg's successors taught Caxton who became the first English master of the mystery a brief 120 years before Shakespeare's first book was printed.

Such an investigation is not inappropriate to professors of analytical bibliography, but it would not in the time available this afternoon bring us very close to the real editorial process in Shakespeare, and it is this process, five hundred years after Caxton, that I should like to discuss with you now. I propose therefore to examine the effect on the editorial tradition created by the issuance this year of four major publications.

These four publications constitute a bumper crop for the workers involved in editing Shakespeare; 1968/69 has been a good year. The harvest is distinguished not only by its quality but by its spirit of international collaboration; British, American, and German scholarship and mechanical ingenuity have worked together as never before. The four publications will be of major significance for the editing of Shakespeare in the years to come. The works themselves have, of course, been in preparation for many years, but their simultaneous appearance in 1968/69 renders the academic year just past an *annus mirabilis* in the textual study of Shakespeare. The year will hereafter be taken, I venture to predict, as the moment that epitomized the transition from old to new in the editing of Shakespeare. The contributions of these works are various, but they all tend toward the establishment of a new authority and away from the pull of the Globe edition. Shakespeare himself had prophesied that

> the great Globe itself,
> Yea, all which it inherit, shall dissolve
> And . . .
> Leave not a rack behind.

The great Globe edition, published just over a century ago, set a standard of editorial acumen, scholarship, and elegance superior to that of any edition that had been published in the 150 years since Nicholas Rowe began the labors of editing Shakespeare, and still remains on balance more generally acceptable than any edition that has been published since.

All modern textual editors are the inheritors of the great Globe, and indeed the two editions of Shakespeare's plays that generally cover the market for undergraduate Shakespeare courses today—those of Hardin Craig and G. B. Harrison—both reprint the Globe text. This fact means clearly and simply that wherever there is a Shakespeare volume on the shelf of any college alumnus, it is very likely to be the Globe text. The late Professor Craig, formerly of The University of North Carolina, which has so graciously extended its hospitality to all of us this summer, wrote in the Preface to the second edition of his *Shakespeare:*

The Globe text has been reprinted with the utmost possible exactitude. The text was chosen for two reasons: first, because the Globe is the model of all complete modern texts and is, by and large, as good as any modern text. . . . The second . . . is that it has been made the principal basis for Shakespearean reference in the modern world. Not only is the line numbering of the Globe text the accepted means of reference, but the text itself has been used in Bartlett's *Concordance to Shakespeare,* the *Oxford English Dictionary,* all Shakespeare grammars and dictionaries, and in literary citation without limit.[5]

Craig speaks for the general and the scholarly reader in regarding the Globe as the stable center of a universe, reverentially circled by modern texts, its dependent satellites. Ptolemy's cosmos is deep in our language, as Professor Nicholson reminded this Institute in 1965,[6] but modern science requires us to shift our metaphor and to see the world through the Tuscan artist's optic tube. Comforted though we no doubt were, we can live no longer in a geocentric universe. The great Globe and all which it inherit are dissolving.

Craig's first reason for continuing the tradition was that the Globe was the model for all subsequent texts and by and large as good as any of them. Critics have for many years had at their disposal several modern editions of Shakespeare's plays as good as the Globe; some of the editors of these texts are luminous indeed: Kittredge, Alexander, Sisson, Dover Wilson, to name a few. Yet these complete editions have not been able to make much of an impression on the general or undergraduate reader, simply because none of them has been generally usable in the undergraduate class (in this country at least).

On April 23, 1969, Professor Alfred Harbage published, as general editor, *William Shakespeare: The Complete Works,* the Pelican Shakespeare.[7] This collaborative edition of American and Canadian scholars for a British firm, designed for the undergraduate class, is by and large as good as the Globe if not better, but it does not follow the Globe model. The edition has many virtues (which I cannot summarize here), but it is unique among editions in disregarding the prominently displayed scene divisions and scene locations of the Globe and of all earlier editions, and in placing inconspicuously to the side the mere scene number. This may seem a small point. But the influence of this salutary change in editorial procedure will be permanent.

The series of individual Pelican texts began in 1956 and

was completed in 1967. Students and readers have therefore been exposed to the new method of scene division in the individual volumes of the series for some years, but the appearance of the new method in the single volume in which all the Pelicans flock together will insure that no modern edition with any pretense to scholarship will be able to present again with impunity elaborate scene headings requiring that we shift our sense of location from "Another part of the Forest" to "Another part of the Forest."[8]

The edition presents for the first time a Shakespearean play in which the modern reader moves from scene to scene without impediment or interruption and with an ease that simulates the lively performance on the Elizabethan stage. The Globe edition was no particular offender in this matter; it merely expressed editorially what nineteenth-century critics were expressing in their writing—that Shakespeare's plays were fitted for the closet not the stage. But as they had originally been written as stage pieces, they had perforce to be presented editorially with the appurtenances of stage movement (entrances and exists). In preparing stage directions for the reader, editors almost without exception visualized the performance of a play designed for Elizabeth as taking place on a stage designed for Victoria.

When in *Romeo and Juliet* the Masquers prepare to "crash" the Capulet party, the Pelican edition reads:

> *Romeo.* . . . But he that hath the steerage of my course
>   Direct my sail! On, lusty gentlemen!
> *Benvolio.* Strike, drum.
>   *They march about the stage, and Servingmen*
>   *come forth with napkins.*
> *1. Servingman.* Where's Potpan that he helps not
>   to take away?[9]

The reader has been moved as the audience has been moved, painlessly and imperceptibly, from the ominous note of Romeo's prayer through the marching and the drum into the below-stairs talk of domestic servants. The Dover Wilson edition explains the transition in a note: "there was no pause or change of scene on Shakespeare's stage. But since we are supposed to pass from the street into Capulet's hall, a change of locality, first marked by Hanmer, is necessary in a reader's text."[10] And that edition reads:

> *Romeo.* . . . But He that hath the steerage of my course
> Direct my sail! On, lusty gentlemen.
> *Benvolio.* Strike, drum. [*they march into the house*
> [1.5]
> *The hall in Capulet's house; musicians waiting.*
> *Enter the masquers, march round the hall, and*
> *stand aside.*
>   '*Servingmen come forth with napkins*'
> *First Servingman.* Where's Potpan, that he helps not
> to take away?

The Dover Wilson reader must visualize the scene on the nineteenth-century stage complete with all its trappings: the Masquers "march into the house," the curtain comes down, the street scene is removed and Capulet's elaborate banqueting hall is hammered into position, the musicians hurry on stage, the curtain rises, the audience returns from casual conversation to the world of illusion (having lost only a part of its dramatic involvement), the Masquers reenter, and the play limps on. It must give us pause to think that the eminent nineteenth-century critics never saw on stage what Shakespeare intended should be seen. A. C. Bradley, who confidently described the dramatic defects of *King Lear,* never saw the play dramatically presented in the theater as Shakespeare intended.

By establishing its own model for scene divisions and locations and by abandoning the Globe model in this conspicuous detail, the Pelican Shakespeare has at once demonstrated that it is a text based on a genuinely new principle and conceived against the background of the Elizabethan theater. In so doing, furthermore, it has called attention to the fact that Shakespeare's plays are plays devised and played to take spectators. It forces upon critics then the importance of editing a play with the stage in mind and that stage the Elizabethan. This achievement may in the long view be the most significant one of this edition.

Craig's second reason for retaining the tradition is that the Globe text has been made the principal basis for Shakespearean reference in the modern world. I do not say that the Pelican text will now become the principal basis for Shakespearean reference in the modern world, but I will say that the Globe text will become less so as the years pass. For our purposes this afternoon, I suggest only that the Pelican sets up a new model in one detail; to other works is left the responsibility of other changes.

On April 23, 1969, Professor Charlton Hinman published *The Norton Facsimile [of] the First Folio of Shakespeare.* This publication on Shakespeare's birthday made available at a moderate cost a thoroughly dependable facsimile, a new, generally acceptable and generally available, principal basis for Shakespearean reference in the modern world.[11]

The Hinman facsimile is the sixth facsimile reproduction of the first folio. The first four of these—published in England in 1886, 1876, 1902, 1909/10—were confined by the smallness of the edition or the loftiness of the price to a limited number of readers and did not gain any popular currency. The fifth of the reproductions—published in New England in 1954—was widely distributed among the reading public through the generosity of the Book of the Month Club.[12] Unhappily, this facsimile never achieved respectability among scholars—one English reviewer crowing over it as a "fake-simile"—and any hopes its editors might have had to establish a new principal basis were disappointed.

Professor Hinman's facsimile is eminently scholarly and thoroughly available. It is therefore possible to say now that any member of the reading public can have at his command the same authority that is respected by Shakespearean scholars everywhere. This happy state existed in 1623 on the original publication of the First Folio, in 1864 when the Globe edition appeared, and has returned to us now in these latter days.

The new facsimile is unique in being a reproduction not

of pages from a single copy but of pages from many copies—thirty, in fact. Professor Hinman worked with the extraordinary collection of First Folios at the Folger Library in Washington and chose for reproduction the clearest example of the fully corrected state of each page in whatever exemplar it was to be found. No facsimile before this one has attempted such an amalgamation of heterogeneous copies, and, indeed almost certainly no copy of the Folio has ever existed in the conditions of correctedness and clarity that this facsimile enjoys. It is "what the printers of the original edition would themselves have considered an ideal copy of the First Folio . . . sufficiently correct for publication."[13]

Craig expanded his second reason for using the Globe by citing two specific virtues: one, the line numbering, and two, the general use of the text itself in the Concordance and in literary citation. The new Hinman facsimile presents a new line-numbering system not modeled after the Globe, but based on the one unassailable, unchanging standard. Professor Hinman writes: "What . . . seems needed, as has long been recognized, is a system of reference which (1) is based on the only edition of the collected works which can reasonably be accepted as a permanent standard, the First Folio; and which (2) numbers the successive typographical lines of this edition, verse and prose and all else alike, straight through each play. This is called 'through line numbering' . . . and this is what is now provided."[14] In the *Prolegomena for the Oxford Shakespeare,* R. B. McKerrow proposed just such a system; that was in 1939. It has now come to pass.

Under the new system of numbering, we shall refer to Hamlet's famous soliloquy, "To be or not to be," as lines 1710–42. This is, I grant, more convenient than the old III.i. 56–88, but I will confess to some private regret in the passing of the old system which gave in addition to the specific line reference a rough idea of where the passage was located dramatically in the play. It is of some use to know that the speech occurs in act three, scene one, and I doubt that we shall come rapidly to an awareness that lines 1646–1848 in *Hamlet* occur in the same dramatic location as act three, scene one.[15] Lines 1710–42 will undoubtedly sound odd to us at first, but as the text of the Globe becomes increasingly less acceptable for reference, the new numbers will become increasingly more acceptable. We live in an age of numbers, it is scarcely necessary to say, and the time may come when we no longer will call the play *Hamlet,* but more accurately No. 32 (it is the thirty-second play in the Folio). The great soliloquy will then become 32.1710–42. Outrageous fortune, indeed.

The Hinman facsimile will accomplish many good works, as we shall see, but it will minimally provide a standard of line reference for Shakespeare designed to replace the Globe numbering. One new popular edition has already begun to appear, utilizing the new lining.[16] The facsimile will not itself provide the text to replace the Globe text, for its readings are raw and still need to be edited to achieve Shakespeare's text, but Professor Hinman will shortly release a new complete edition of Shakespeare with the through-line numbering.[17]

Craig cited the general use of the Globe text in works of reference, specifically in Bartlett's *Concordance to Shakespeare.* Since 1895 Bartlett's *Concordance* has been the constant companion and *vade mecum* of Shakespeare scholars. Based on the Globe text, it has been an irreplaceable reference work. It has now been replaced by a new Concordance based on a new text —not the Globe.

In 1968, Professor Marvin Spevack, an American scholar working at a German university and with German equipment, published the first three volumes of a computer-generated *Complete and Systematic Concordance to the Works of Shakespeare.* The Preface states that the concordance is based on the text of *The Works of Shakespeare,* soon to be published by the Houghton Mifflin Co.: "A new, advanced, complete, and easily accessible one-volume work."[18] The references are to a new system of line numbering—not the Globe: "independent of the old counting." The first three volumes are a statistician's paradise: the word is given, and all the rest numbers; the last three volumes will provide also the context (in the time-honored, more leisurely Bartlett fashion). Professor Spevack describes his "complete and accurate computer-generated concordance to all of Shakespeare" thus:

> The work consists of a series of interlocking concordances to the individual plays, to the characters, to the poems (singly and together), and to the complete works—in which all the words are indexed in exactly the form in which they appear in the text of Shakespeare, together with primary statistical data, as well as the indication of homographs and departures from the respective copy-texts.
>
> The first three volumes contain concordances to the individual dramas and characters in the Folio order. . . . The last three volumes . . . contain a concordance to the complete works with cumulative statistical information, a context for each word, an index of all the words arranged according to frequency of occurrence, and a complete list of homographs.
>
> At the beginning of the concordance to each drama, general statistical information is provided: the total number of speeches, the number in verse, in prose, in a mixture of verse and prose; the total number of lines, the number in verse, in prose, the number of split lines; the total number of words, the number in verse, in prose, the number of different words.
>
> Then each word is given . . . together with its absolute frequency within the drama . . . its relative frequency . . . its occurrence in verse contexts . . . its occurrence in prose . . . and its location. . . .
>
> Immediately following each drama concordance is a concordance to the vocabulary of its characters or speaking roles. . . . For each speaking role general statistical information similar in nature to that for the drama is provided, followed by the percentage of the total speeches, lines, and words of the drama which a particular character speaks.[19]

The new Concordance will be enormously helpful in working with Shakespeare's language; where before we have had a complete record of every word used by Shakespeare, we now have a complete record of every word used by Hamlet or by Claudius, by Richard II or by Bolingbroke. This new kind of analysis, it may be noted, addresses itself to the dramatic context and helps us to see the work as a play rather than a poem.

"In *Hamlet,*" Professor Spevack informs us, explaining the advantages of the Concordance to a character's speeches, "the most frequent word after the so-called 'insignificant' ones and just a few of the most common verbs is *Hamlet* (85 times) : by Claudius 28 times; by Gertrude 17. Of the words Hamlet himself speaks, assuming the same exceptions as above, the most frequent is *man*—Hamlet's 36 uses accounting for more than 60 percent of the play's total of 57. Stylistic, linguistic, and cultural insights are suggested by the striking occurrence of such words in this play as might otherwise escape notice— *very, as, what, o, sir,* to mention but a few. In fact, the so-called 'insignificant' words provide such rich possibilities in the study of Shakespeare and early modern English that they too are given, for the first and only time anywhere, with complete statistical information and a complete context."[20]

I said a moment ago that we have had in Bartlett's Concordance a complete record of every word used by Shakespeare. That confidence seems now to have been ill-supported. Bartlett records 30 uses of the word "chain" in the *Comedy of Errors*—the word is a fairly important one in the texture of the dialogue, in the intricacy of the plot, and in the representation of the dramatic object. Professor Spevack calls attention to the fact that he records 45 uses—half again as many.[21] It is a sobering consideration, but my own examination indicates that it is not the average for the whole work. Bartlett's efficiency improved as he progressed through the Folio, and the *Comedy of Errors* is fairly early in the volume. Even so, the greater accuracy and completeness of the new Concordance will require its use in many critical and editorial problems, and its basic text will surely supplant the Globe text in Bartlett.

The fourth major publication of the year is so new that it has arrived only very recently at libraries in this country. It is the Trevor Howard-Hill series, *Oxford Old-spelling Concordances.*[22] These Concordances are based on the First Folio, or on the first substantive quarto for appropriate texts, and the work uses Professor Hinman's through-line numbering. It is another joint Anglo-American undertaking. The Concordances are being published separately play-by-play; the five comedies first in the Folio are just now in hand.

Having lived for three quarters of a century on the solitary delights of one Bartlett Concordance (and one not complete or accurate, it appears), we are now able to rejoice in two different new Concordances to Shakespeare's works. We may feel tempted to cry with Portia,

> Be moderate; . . . scant this excess. . . .
> I feel too much thy blessing: make it less
> For fear I surfeit.

But we shall not surfeit, for the two Concordances are supplementary, not duplicating. On the basis of these two works we may look to see for the next fifty years of Shakespearean scholarship two streams of editorial criticism: the one grounded in the Houghton Mifflin edition and Spevack's Concordance will be literary; the other grounded in the First Folio and Howard-Hill's Concordances will be analytical.

Before speaking of the major achievement of these Oxford Concordances, I might mention one of their subordinate virtues. Like other Concordances, these provide a record of the text, of course, but they provide also a record of the stage directions in the original edition. This information will be of great value (when it is all assembled) to students of staging, and it too will nourish the growing and essential interest in the play as a stage representation on Elizabeth's stage. Such information is not available elsewhere in any form.[23]

The Oxford Concordances, however, will serve their chief function by supplying textual critics with an almost instantaneous analysis of the spelling habits of the compositors of the early editions of the plays. The Concordances are properly appearing by play individually, because compositorial analysis proceeds play by play, though there are plans to program them later into a single alphabet. The Concordance to *Merry Wives* for example tells us that the verb form "been" appears 26 times in the play: as *been* one time, as *beene* sixteen times, as *bene* twice, as *bin* seven times. It further tells us which of these spellings might have been influenced by the length of the line of type in the Folio. Each volume contains also the assignment of shares in the composition by folio column to each of the five compositors as far as is now known. It is therefore the matter of a moment to assemble the richest imaginable amount of information on the spellings of the various compositors for any column of any folio page.

It will not, I hasten to add, be the matter of a moment to evaluate this mass of material—therein the editor must minister to himself. The computer is only the handmaiden of analytical bibliography, just as analytical bibliography is the handmaiden of literary criticism.

On the studies made possible by these Oxford Concordances —to move into the future—the finally definitive, critical text of Shakespeare will be based. By knowing thoroughly the spelling patterns and variable practices of the compositors of a particular play, editors should be able with a reasonable degree of probability to reconstruct the original spellings used by Shakespeare and so to reconstitute, as it were, the lost manuscript of Shakespeare himself. For those plays in which a scribal transcript intervenes between the holograph and the print the task will be more difficult, but something may be said even of them. This hypothetical, recovered or reconstituted manuscript will be the finally definitive text of Shakespeare, in Shakespeare's own spelling.

Every reprint of a Shakespeare play—beginning even with the first—has modernized the spelling, has attempted to make Shakespeare look like a modern. But as modern textual scholarship in the early twentieth century grew to maturity and developed more exact critical standards, it became evident that a modern-spelling edition of Shakespeare was inadequate for its purposes. Accordingly, F. J. Furnivall, W. G. Boswell-Stone, and F. W. Clarke began a series called *The Old-Spelling Shakespeare* and published seventeen plays from 1907 to 1912.[24] These plays might have been influential in the history of editing Shakespeare; they were not. Perhaps it was that the series was never finished. Boswell-Stone died early in the work, Furnivall in 1910; and the publisher did not continue the series. In 1930, Sir Edmund Chambers wrote "A text in Elizabethan spelling is still a *desideratum.*"[25] Shortly thereafter, the Oxford University Press requested R. B. McKerrow to edit an old-spelling text of Shakespeare. McKerrow undertook the task, but all his health allowed him to produce was the *Prolegomena for the Oxford Shakespeare* in 1939.[26] Since the war, two distinguished British scholars have successively been invited to continue the edition, but nothing has as yet appeared. Some years ago, the *Times Literary Supplement* was so rash as to carry an advance notice of the publication of the first volume of the edition, *Coriolanus;* the notice has not yet been followed by the fact. Professor Harbage in the Introduction to the Pelican Shakespeare writes: "An old-spelling edition utilizing modern advances in textual study remains a desideratum."[27]

I have spoken of the publication of four works of major significance to the transmission of Shakespeare's text during the past academic year. I can add another publishing event of some significance in its own small way: in June, 1969, Messrs. Scott, Foresman contracted to produce in Spring, 1970, the first old-spelling text of a Shakespeare play in a format designed for the American undergraduate or general reader. It is to be hoped that this tentative (not to say risky) venture will receive sufficient support from the public and from undergraduate classes that the publishers will be persuaded to produce the entire corpus in old spelling. The projected series will be under the supervision of Professor Robert K. Turner, Jr., of the University of Wisconsin in Milwaukee.

The edition will utilize modern advances in textual study, will suggest a staging in terms of the Elizabethan stage, will have the new through-line numbering, and will provide literary glosses and the usual assistance for the undergraduate reader. If it has any popular currency, the series will go far in bridging the gaps between old editorial practices and new, and between restricted scholarship and popular consumption.

The Scott, Foresman edition in old spelling will be a transitional text, not the finally definitive text of Shakespeare, yet its appearance following soon upon the Hinman facsimile does seem to be timely. Still, lest we become too smug, let me read the publishers' blurb for the Furnivall *Old-Spelling Shakespeare* in 1910:

The project of issuing an edition of Shakespeare in such a form as would have harmonized with the poet's own orthography has engaged Dr. Furnivall's attention and entailed much active work on his part for more than a quarter of a century. In the enthusiasm which has lately been evoked by the successful launching of costly reproductions of the Shakespeare Folios, Dr. Furnivall has had the good fortune to realize that his has not been a voice crying unheard. His untiring advocacy of the principle that scholars should have Shakespeare's text before them as nearly as possible in the exact form in which it left Shakespeare's own hand, is now becoming universally accepted.

So much for the vanity of human wishes. Dr. Furnivall's voice, *clamans in deserto,* was unheard; his edition was only halfway through when it was discontinued. Let us yet hope, that after sixty years Dr. Furnivall's principle is finally now becoming universally accepted.

Furnivall's failure demonstrated that the world was not ready for an old-spelling edition, yet the plaints of Chambers and Professor Harbage speak to the continuing desire for such an edition. Surely, if the perfect text does exist, it exists in old spelling. The functions of an old-spelling edition published now are two, I take it: to accustom the reader to the concept of old spelling (at least on the college or university level) and to provide him with a more authoritative text before that finally definitive vision is realized.

Addressing himself to an audience of scholars, Professor Fredson Bowers explained the nature of the old spelling text in "Today's Shakespeare Texts, and Tomorrow's."[28] He asked why an old-spelling edition was more authoritative in its form than a modernized text. And he replied that in practice, "The modernizing editor works basically at secondhand, without the minute and scrupulous examination of the source materials that marks the activities of the old spelling editor." In principle, the virtues are clearer and more positive: "For old-spelling texts the original evidence is revealed to the reader,

[75]

with no impenetrable screen of silent editorial decision con-
cealing from him the essential facts."[29] Professor Bowers cited
three specific disadvantages of the modern-spelling edition as
opposed to the old-spelling: the ambiguity involved in the
use of the genitive apostrophe, the loss of puns or word-plays
in modern spelling, the reshaping of Shakespearean punctuation
that must accompany the modern spelling.

In 1961, I prepared (by offset) for my undergraduate
classes an old-spelling edition of *Romeo and Juliet;* I used this
edition for several years—until the distributed copies no longer
returned in sufficient quantity to be distributed again. The
Introduction designed for the students using that edition
spoke to the same point made by Professor Bowers, it read
in part:

The philosophy of the editing of Elizabethan plays for the
general reader is in the process of a remarkable change. Editors
of the eighteenth, nineteenth, and early twentieth centuries consistently sought to recreate the forms and format of a play in the
image of their own times. They regularized and made uniform
the variables which characterized a less disciplinary age. Within
the past few decades, however, some editors instead of trying to
bring the play up to the present have wished to take the reader
back to the past; hence, one by one the rigorous impositions of
earlier editors have been and are being cleared from the text.
Editors now recognize that the Elizabethan stage was different
from the modern stage; in consequence, editions now appear without descriptive locations and elaborate stage directions. Editors
now accept the fact that Elizabethan punctuation—appalling by
nineteenth-century standards—served its purpose quite adequately;
in consequence, effectiveness is taking the place of exactness. Editors have discovered that the Elizabethans had a more broad-
minded approach to the rules of grammar than was customary in
the eighteenth century; in consequence, what appear to be dis-
agreements between subject and verb, erroneous references of
pronouns, and like "mistakes" are accepted as the idiom proper
to the age. Only normalized spelling—the invention of the printers
and the lexicographers—has resisted the trend from formality to
freedom. The present edition takes the final step in the process
by restoring the spelling in which the play first made its appearance
in print. The spelling is appropriate to the temper of the play;

it is in harmony with the age; it is the spelling which Shakespeare would have recognized; it is in a large measure the spelling that Shakespeare wrote. The editor who obliterates any aspect of the creative imagination of his author—even though in so small a detail as spelling—commits an offense against the serious student.

The student without specialized training may inquire what virtue there is in reading Shakespeare "in the original." Surely, he will say, the problems of interpretation are difficult enough of themselves; why should the additional barrier of a strange spelling be placed between him and the mind of the dramatist? The answer lies in this: the barrier is imaginary. The only real barrier that old spelling raises is that of novelty. Once the reader has grown accustomed to the forms—as he will after a very few pages—the barrier disappears, and he makes his approach to the spirit of the author and his time with a directness not before available.

Analytical bibliographers have from the earliest days of the mystery been optimistic. Sir Walter Greg and J. Dover Wilson both spoke glowingly of the enthusiasm, the encouragement, and the inspiration of the first grand master, Alfred W. Pollard. McKerrow felt that the future was almost within his grasp and that analytical bibliography could solve eventually any textual problem placed before it. The science has been marked by a continuing hope and cheerfulness in the face of the most awful amount of drudgery, because always at the end of the tunnel has been the possibility of seeing Shakespeare plain. I must confess to having caught some of that vision and some of that excitement in this critical year. I am confident that in later years the conjunction of starry events of 1968/69 will be seen as marking the moment at which the editing of Shakespeare left the Globe behind and took the first step into the universe of new principles. Textual critics can now feel themselves watchers of the skies as, eagle-eyed, they approach nearer and nearer to the essential sun of Shakespeare. It is a moment that calls for a Keats—and the same sense of wonder with which he turned from Pope's translation of Homer to look into Chapman's—to record the future reader's sense of clarity and penetration as he turns from old texts to new texts of Shakespeare and breathes that pure serene.

[77]

NOTES

1. Arthur Brown, "The Transmission of the Text," in *Medieval and Renaissance Studies*, ed. John L. Lievsay (Durham, 1968).

2. The A. S. W. Rosenbach Fellowship in Bibliography (Philadelphia: University of Pennsylvania Library, 1955); reprinted with additional papers as *On Editing Shakespeare* (Charlottesville, 1966).

3. A. van der Linde, *The Haarlem Legend of the Invention of Printing . . . Critically Examined* (London, 1871).

4. O. W. Fuhrmann, *Gutenberg and the Strasbourg Documents of 1439* (New York, 1940).

5. Hardin Craig, *Shakespeare*, rev. ed. (Chicago, 1958), p. iv.

6. Marjorie Nicholson, "The Discovery of Space," in *Medieval and Renaissance Studies*, ed. O. B. Hardison, Jr. (Chapel Hill, 1966), p. 42.

7. Alfred Harbage, ed., *William Shakespeare: The Complete Works* (Baltimore, 1969).

8. See for example, W. J. Craig, ed. *As You Like It* [*The Oxford Shakespeare*] (Oxford, n.d.), II. v, vi, vii; or more recently, Leonard Nathanson, ed., *The Tempest* [*The Blackfriars Shakespeare*] (Dubuque, 1969), "Another part of the island," II. i, ii; III. ii, iii.

9. John E. Hankins, ed., *Romeo and Juliet* [*Pelican Shakespeare*] (Baltimore, 1969), p. 866.

10. Dover Wilson and G. I. Duthie, eds., *Romeo and Juliet* [*Cambridge New Shakespeare*] (Cambridge, 1955), pp. 144–45, 23.

11. Charlton Hinman, ed., *The Norton Facsimile* [*of*] *the First Folio of Shakespeare* (New York, 1968). The Deluxe Edition appeared in October, 1968; the Academic Edition in April, 1969. The differences between the two editions (i.e., issues) are confined to quality of paper and binding.

12. Another facsimile (reduced)—The Dallastype Shakespeare—was begun in 1893 but did not proceed beyond the Preliminaries and the first four plays (the British Museum has an incomplete set). The project was superseded in 1895 by the Double Text Dallastype Shakespeare which printed the folio page in facsimile facing the equivalent text edited by Charles Knight; it was not completed. In 1928 J. Dover Wilson published in individual volumes facsimiles of ten plays of which the authoritative first editions were in the First Folio.

13. Hinman, *Facsimile,* pp. xxii-xxiii.

14. *Ibid.,* p. xxiv.

15. I should myself have preferred a system in which the scenes were numbered consecutively—one through twenty in *Hamlet*, for example; the soliloquy would then be cited as viii. 56–88. But this is a private interest of mine and may be subject to more confusion than the through line numbering.

16. J. Leeds Barroll, ed., *The Blackfriars Shakespeare* (Dubuque, Iowa).

17. The edition is to be published by W. W. Norton & Co., Inc.

18. Marvin Spevack, *Complete and Systematic Concordance to the Works of Shakespeare* (Hildesheim, 1968), p. x.

19. *Ibid.,* pp. vii-viii.

20. Marvin Spevack, "A New Shakespeare Concordance: Research Opportunities," *Shakespeare Newsletter,* XIX (February, 1969), 8.

21. *Ibid.*

22. Trevor Howard-Hill, *Oxford Old-spelling Concordances* (Oxford, 1971).

23. Since this paper was delivered, Professor Spevack has announced his

intention to present the quarto and folio directions in a forthcoming volume (*Concordance,* p. 4340).

24. F. J. Furnivall et al., *The Old-Spelling Shakespeare* (London, 1907–12).

25. E. K. Chambers, *William Shakespeare* (Oxford, 1930), I, 276.

26. R. B. McKerrow, *Prolegomena for the Oxford Shakespeare* (Oxford, 1939).

27. Harbage, ed., *William Shakespeare,* p. 45. Since this paper was delivered, the University of South Carolina Press has announced the publication of an old-spelling Shakespeare to be under the general editorship of J. Leeds Barroll; in England, Messrs. Ginn & Co., Ltd., are publishing by offset from typescript an old-spelling series of Shakespeare's best-known plays.

28. Fredson Bowers, "Today's Shakespeare Texts, and Tomorrow's," in *Studies in Bibliography,* XIX (1966), 39–65.

29. *Ibid.,* pp. 51, 52.

IV

The Revival of Antiquity in Early Renaissance Sculpture

H. W. Janson
New York University

In his *Treatise on Painting,* Leonardo da Vinci at one point advises the painter to look at stained walls, varicolored stones, clouds, or the ashes of a fire, as an aid to invention.[1] "You can see there," he says, "resemblances to . . . landscapes . . . battles . . . strange expressions on faces," which can become the starting point of pictorial designs. "This happens . . . as in the sound of bells, in whose pealing you can find every name and word you can imagine." Surely Leonardo was not the first to observe that (as the nursery rhyme has it) "Oranges and lemons/Say the bells of St. Clement's," although he may well have been the first to refer to the phenomenon in writing. Be that as it may, I often think that classical antiquity has the quality of Leonardo's bells, inviting later ages to find in it whatever they want to find. I sometimes wonder whether it might not be worth while to establish an anti-Warburg Institute, devoted to the cataloguing of ideas and traditions that can definitely be shown *not* to be of classical origin. If we were to do that, we should of course have to start by defining what we mean by classical antiquity. We could not, I believe, afford to tackle the impossible job of singling out what we might choose to call the "classical aspects" of Graeco-Roman civilization; we should have to concern ourselves with all of that civilization, from the time of the Doric migrations to the final collapse of the Roman Empire in the West—a span of nearly 1,500 years in the course of which the Greeks and Romans absorbed not only the territories but also the cultural traditions of most of the ancient Near East. This adds up to a vast and varied "sound of bells" (if I may revert once more to Leonardo's simile). To be sure, not all the bells were audible at all times, but in the aggregate they have never stopped pealing, and people have never ceased to listen for the "names and words" they wanted to hear.

It is, needless to say, necessary and instructive to locate the bells that were going at a given time and in a given place. Was this or that classical text available then, and if so, in what form? Was this or that ancient work of art visible as a potential model? Such is the purpose of the Census of Antique Works of Art known to the Renaissance, which has been growing ever since 1949 under the joint sponsorship of the Institute of Fine Arts at New York University and the Warburg Institute. But this "locating of the bells" more often than not is a frustrating and uncertain procedure. Until we get to comparatively recent times, i.e., the seventeenth century, the instances when we can say with assurance that a specific text or work of art was rediscovered in such-and-such a year after having been lost since late antiquity are few and far between. How can we be certain that another example, perhaps one that failed to survive until the present day, was not known before the supposed rediscovery? The chances of this having happened vary greatly and must be carefully appraised in every single case. There are, of course, some bells—a small fraction of the total but nevertheless a sizable number—of which we know that they sounded throughout the Middle Ages and the Renaissance, such as Pliny's *Natural History* or the equestrian statue of Marcus Aurelius in Rome. These in particular, it seems to me, bear out the analogy I used in my opening remarks; for they spoke differently to every age. Pliny's chapters on the visual arts and the architectural treatise of Vitruvius are a good case in point. Certain passages in them have been cited in order to account for such novel Renaissance phenomena as the notion of "artistic progress," the rise of landscape painting as a genre in its own right, and the appreciation of unfinished works such as drawings and sketches.[2] All this is certainly illuminating; but why did these same passages fall on deaf ears in the Middle Ages? Once people were ready to appreciate drawings and sketches they were surely pleased to find that according to Pliny certain painters in antiquity were more highly esteemed for their sketches than for their finished works, because the sketches showed the workings of the artist's mind. Yet this hardly justifies the claim that the Pliny passage kindled the Renaissance collector's enthusiasm for unfinished works. On the other hand, is it not true that the Renaissance read Pliny with more attention and respect than did the Middle Ages? Otherwise we should find it hard to differentiate the Renaissance from the various classical revivals of medieval times. Perhaps, then, the Pliny passage did play a significant role in stimulating the Renaissance collector's interest in drawings and sketches.

Such may indeed be the case in our particular instance, but the Renaissance way of listening to the sound of the classical bells was by no means invariably superior to the medieval way. The classical attitude toward the visual arts may serve as a test case. To the ancients, painting and sculpture were crafts, mechanical arts rather than liberal arts, and the notion of a painter or sculptor of genius would have struck most of them as absurd; genius—or inspiration, to use an alternative term—was reserved for the poet. Strange as this low ranking of the fine arts may seem in view of the towering achievements of ancient artists, it is attested by the overwhelming majority of classical thinkers, from Plato to Seneca and Plotinus. And the Middle Ages faithfully accepted their verdict. It was the Renaissance, beginning in Florence around 1400, that sought to promote painting and sculpture to liberal-arts status.[3] Needless to say, the claim had to be buttressed with evidence drawn from classical sources, but such evidence was hard to come by. It is astounding to observe the intellectual acrobatics by which this feat was accomplished, disregarding all arguments to the contrary. Thus we read that painting must be a liberal art because Alexander the Great rewarded Apelles with his favorite mistress and because Nero is said to have been a painter. The humanists might of course have argued that if painting and sculpture had been mechanical arts in antiquity they were liberal arts *now;* but that would have demolished the authority of ancient art as a guide for modern artists, hence the argument would be self-defeating.

Leone Battista Alberti faced a similar conflict when, in his treatise on architecture, he claimed that the ideal plan of a temple (by which he meant any house of god, pagan or Christian) was round, polygonal, or square, rather than rectangular.[4] The Christian basilica, he argued, had originally served a secular purpose and thus could not be expected to conform to the ideal, unlike the Pantheon in Rome. Yet it could hardly have escaped Alberti that the vast majority of ancient temples were rectangular in plan, and that the Pantheon and the handful of smaller round temples in or near Rome were the exception rather than the rule. In these cases, then, and in many similar ones, the Renaissance heard "liberal arts" and "round" when the bells were actually saying "mechanical arts" and "rectangular." To differentiate the revival of antiquity in the Renaissance from the various medieval revivals can thus be a rather delicate matter at times. Yet I have not the least desire to abolish the Renaissance as a historic period, or even to defend my not wanting to abolish it. My cautionary remarks are intended merely to suggest that my subject is a difficult one, perhaps even more so in the visual arts than in literature or philosophy. For that reason, I propose to limit my remarks to Florentine sculpture, and to the first half of the Quattrocento, so as to permit a reasonably full discussion of the instances I want to examine.

Panofsky has defined the difference between the Renaissance and the medieval renascences of ancient art as "the reintegration of classical form and content." In the Middle Ages, the two were oddly dissociated: a medieval artist might copy, let us say, a statue of Venus, but in doing so he would give it a new identity such as one of the Cardinal Virtues, while if he wanted to represent the goddess Venus he would

[83]

visualize her as a courtly lady in modern dress. Not until the Quattrocento in Italy—as we all know from the famous picture by Botticelli—did Venus regain her classical appearance. This process of reintegration, however, took place mainly during the second half of the century. If we were to seek a similar formula for the first half, we might say that it is characterized by the imposition of classical form on non-classical subjects which had escaped this process during the Middle Ages. We shall see several instances of this. Once we have settled on the first half of the Quattrocento, the further limitation to Florence is almost implicit; while Florence was not the only home of early Renaissance art during those decades, it was its original home, and its position of leadership was undisputed.

But why concentrate on sculpture only? There are several good reasons. First of all, early Renaissance art began with sculpture. If we imagine ourselves visiting Florence in 1420, we could have seen the new style embodied in a number of statues and reliefs, but not yet in any buildings or pictures. This is, needless to say, mainly the achievement of Donatello, the founding father of Renaissance sculpture. Still, it was not his individual genius alone that accounts for the priority of sculpture. Here we may recall the title of the earliest Renaissance treatise on art, Alberti's *De Statua* of about 1430, probably written in Rome while the author was in contact with Donatello. Why did Alberti write on sculpture before he wrote on painting or architecture? And why did he call his treatise "On the Statue"? He did so, I suspect, because statues—that is, free-standing images in the round—are as characteristic of ancient sculpture as they are alien to the Middle Ages. It was on free-standing statues that the early Church had centered its wrath as pagan idols *par excellence* and the dwelling places of demons. Countless numbers of them were destroyed as Christianization spread through the Roman Empire. And the conviction that statues are the seats of demons—which is simply the negative counterpart of the worship formerly accorded to them as the seats of the gods—persisted throughout the Middle Ages. In order to serve a Christian purpose, sculpture in the

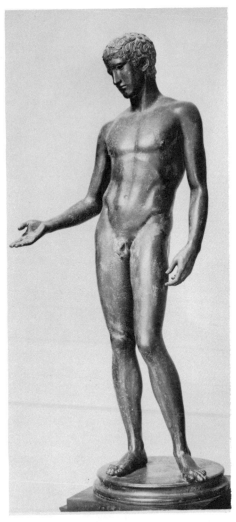

1. Donatello, *David*, c. 1430
(Bargello, Florence)

2. *Idolino* (Archaeological Museum,
Florence)

3. *Thorn-Puller* (Capitoline Museum, Rome)

4. Donatello, *Dancing Angel*, 1429 (Baptismal Font, S. Giovanni, Siena)

5. Etruscan Bronze Vessel, Detail (Archaeological Museum, Bologna)

6. *Hadrian* (Uffizi, Florence)

7. Antonio Rossellino, *Giovanni Chellini,* 1456 (Victoria and Albert Museum, London [Crown copyright])

8. *Marcus Aurelius* (Archaeological Museum, Lausanne)

9. Side View of Fig. 8

10. Head Reliquary of St. Alexander, Completed 1145 (Royal Museum, Brussels)

11. *Sainte-Foy*, Ninth to Tenth Century, the Head Late Roman (Abbey Treasury, Conques)

12. Head Reliquary of St. Ursula, Early Fourteenth Century (Historisches Museum, Basel)

13. Donatello, Reliquary Bust of St. Rossore, c. 1425 (Museo di San Matteo, Pisa)

5. Donatello, *Beardless Prophet*
1416-18 (Cathedral Museum,
Florence)

16. Donatello, So-Called *Jeremiah*,
1427–35 (Cathedral Museum,
Florence)

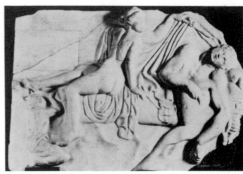

18. *Bed of Policlitus,* Private Collection

14. Aquamanile, Early Thirteenth Century (Domkapitel, Aachen)

17. Tombstone of Quintus Sulpicius Maximus, Detail (Museo Nuovo Capitolino, Rome)

19. Donatello, *Feast of Herod,* Detail, c. 1435 (Musée Wicar, Lille)

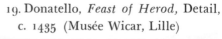

20. Donatello, *Apotheosis of St. John the Evangelist,* c. 1435 (Old Sacristy, S. Lorenzo, Florence)

22. *Marcus Aurelius Distributing Largesse* (Arch of Constantine, Rome)

21. Giotto, *Apotheosis of St. John the Evangelist,* c. 1325 (S. Croce, Florence)

23. Donatello, *Assumption of the Virgin*, 1427-28 (S. Angelo a Nilo, Naples)

24. Andrea Orcagna, *Assumption of the Virgin*, c. 1359, Or San Michele (Florence)

26. Sarcophagus, Sixth Century
(Archaeological Museum,
Istanbul)

25. *Assumption of the Virgin,* From
MS No. 40, f. 225r. c. 1280 (Museo
Diocesano, Pistoia)

27. Sarcophagus, Detail (Villa
Medici, Rome)

30. Mosaic in the Vault of the Scarsella, Det
Thirteenth Century (Baptistery, Florence)

29. Silver Box Lid with the
Marriage of Atys and Cybele,
Detail (Brera, Milan)

28. Sarcophagus of Junius Bassus, Detail,
c. 359 (Vatican Grottoes, Rome)

31. Donatello, Equestrian Monument of Gattamelata, 1447-53 (Piazza del Santo, Padua)

32. Equestrian Statue of Marcus Aurelius (Piazza del Campidoglio, Rome)

33. Pedestal of the Equestrian Monument of Niccolò d'Este, c. 1450 (Ferrara)

34. *Regisole,* Woodcut from *Statuta Papie,* 1505

35. Equestrian Statue of Philip the
Fair, Engraving, 1575

36. Tomb of Can Grande della Scala,
1329 (S. Maria Antica, Verona)

37. Tomb of Guglielmo Berardi, 1289
(SS. Annunziata, Florence)

38. Tomb of Paolo Savelli,
1405 (S. Maria dei Frari,
Venice)

39. Tomb of Cortesia
Sarego, 1432
(S. Anastasia, Verona)

. Donatello, Equestrian Monument of Gattamelata, Detail

41. *Marcus Holconius Rufus*
(National Museum, Naples)

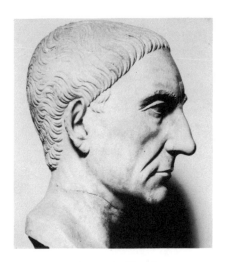

43. Roman Portrait Head
(Vatican Museums, Rome)

42. Donatello, Equestrian Monument of Gattamelata, Detail

round had to be "de-activated" by becoming attached (and thus subordinate) to the architectural framework of the House of God or its furnishings, such as pulpits and choir screens. Hence Alberti must have felt, and quite rightly, that there could be no rebirth of antiquity in art without the revival of the free-standing statue. The stages by which Donatello and others accomplished this between 1410 and 1430 need not detain us here. Let us turn, rather, to Donatello's bronze *David* of about 1430 (Fig. 1), the earliest surviving lifesize example, and very probably the first free-standing statue made since the end of antiquity. It would retain this claim even if it were not nude, but its nudity lends special emphasis to its classical qualities, since it brings to mind all the nude statues of youths in Greek and Roman art (Fig. 2). There is the same balanced and self-sufficient stance, the same sensuous beauty of form. However, as soon as we compare the *David* with specific examples of ancient nude youths, we begin to realize how different Donatello's figure is. His forms are leaner, more angular, nor has he taken over the classical formulae for subdividing the torso but has, to all appearances, worked from the living model. (It may not be irrelevant here to recall that he had the reputation of always chasing after beautiful apprentices.)[5] There is indeed no reason to believe that any statues of nude youths were accessible to him; all those we have today were discovered later, with the single exception of the *Thorn-Puller* (Fig. 3) which was visible in Rome throughout the Middle Ages but could at best have furnished the idea, not the concrete model for Donatello's statue. Small bronzes, on the other hand, were easily available, especially those of Etruscan manufacture such as could often be found in Etruscan tombs. We know that these tombs were opened and their contents appreciated in Donatello's day.[6] The link can be proved, I think, if we turn to the three nude *Putti* Donatello did in the late 1420's for the baptismal font in Siena (Fig. 4). They are the immediate predecessors of the *David*, with whom they share the circular base (a wreath in both cases) and the fact that they stand on an uneven surface (a scallop shell in Siena, Goliath's head in the *David*). Why should an artist have complicated his task in this fashion when experimenting with free-standing figures for the first time, instead of adopting the straight horizontal plinth of classical statues? I suggest that the idea came to Donatello from looking at Etruscan bronze statuettes attached to vases and cysts, unique in ancient art for their precarious perch on sloping surfaces (Fig. 5). These bronze vessels ornamented with statuettes were produced in large numbers; many hundreds of them still exist today. He may very well, therefore, have known figures similar to our example. The lively movement of the Siena *Putto* also seems to have been suggested by the same source.[7] In the *David,* the movement has disappeared, but another Etruscan feature persists: both figures, though nude, are wearing boots. To a Greek, or to a Roman, this would have appeared incongruous, while in Etruscan art the "booted nude" is far from rare. If we are right in assuming that no large-scale standing nude statue was available to Donatello as a model for his *David*—and so far no evidence has come to light to gainsay us—we begin to understand why he arrived at so original a solution. Had a large-scale model been at his disposal, he might well have produced something more conventionally "correct" by ancient standards but far less striking as a work of art.

Another species of ancient sculpture that had lapsed during the Middle Ages was revived in the early Renaissance—the portrait bust. This, too, was long thought to have been an achievement of Donatello, but it turns out not to be. The earliest specimens we know were made by younger sculptors in Florence in the 1450's. Apparently the revival of the portrait bust occurred during the decade 1443–53, which Donatello spent in Padua. In the art historical literature, it has always been treated as a simple case of picking up where the Romans left off. Yet when we compare any Roman bust (Fig. 6) with a fifteenth-century example such as the *Giovanni Chellini* of 1456 by Antonio Rossellino (Fig. 7) it becomes apparent that the process could not have been as straightforward as that. Rossellino undoubtedly knew Roman busts—we know they were collected as early as the mid-fifteenth century—but the differences are as striking as the similarities.[8] Rossellino's bust looks like a statue cut off at a point midway between the shoulder and the elbow, while in the Roman specimen the chest is treated as a sort of bib attached to the neck. This somewhat irreverent description must be allowed to stand for the moment, since it takes in all the essentials of the Roman solution: the chest is a hollow, sloping shield, which demands that the bust be placed on a special stand or foot, while the early Renaissance bust can be set directly on any horizontal surface. The "bib" can be seen more clearly in the front and side views of a bust of Marcus Aurelius (Figs. 8, 9); here the stand has been lost, but the piece obviously required one. This bust is of special interest to us. It was found in Avenches, a large Roman military camp in Switzerland, and the precious material—beaten gold—suggests that it was a cult image for the emperor worship of the Roman legions. There must have been many such gold busts, although for obvious reasons few have come down to us.[9] Oddly enough, however, it was these, rather than the far more common marble busts, that survived after a fashion in medieval art. They are the ancestors of a widespread class of medieval sculpture: the head reliquary, i.e., a head made of beaten gold or silver (or gilt or silvered copper) as a container for the scull of a saint, such as that of *Pope Alexander* in Brussels (Fig. 10). Despite its early-twelfth-century date, this head retains some distinctly Roman features.[10] In another instance, the link with the gold busts of Roman emperors is clearer still; the gold statue of *Sainte-Foy* in Conques (Fig. 11), the most elaborate of all reliquaries, has a head which turns out to be that of a late Roman emperor, cut off at the neck and re-used for the head of a female saint.[11] Apparently *Sainte-Foy* started out as a head reliquary, with the rest of the body added somewhat later. Returning for a moment to *Pope Alexander,* we note that the head rests on a jeweled box. In Gothic head reliquaries such as that of *St. Ursula* in Basel (Fig. 12) the box and head merge, and we now have a bust of the early Renaissance type, rather than of the "bib" type. The final link between these reliquary busts and *Giovanni Chellini* is Donatello's *St. Rossore* of about 1425 (Fig. 13), in which the shoulders and chest have been given their proper size in relation to the head and the features are so individual that it might almost pass for a portrait. The early Renaissance bust might thus be termed a secularized reliquary; its revival-of-antiquity aspect consists of the use of marble in place of precious metal, of the realistic facial geography, and of the fact that it represents a living individual. This type proved extraordinarily persistent; not until the sixteenth century do we find a resumption of the "bib" type in Renaissance portrait busts. Why it proved so persistent is a difficult question which I cannot attempt to answer here.[12] To humanistically schooled patrons, who had read in classical sources about Roman ancestor worship and the *imagines maiorum* kept in a special shrine in Roman houses and displayed in funerary processions, these portraits may well have had an odor of "pagan sanctity," so that their shape, recalling reliquary busts, had exactly the right connotations.[13]

The evolutionary sequence outlined above also throws an interesting light on the medieval attitude toward sculpture in the round; the imperial gold busts were, after all, not only sculpture in the round but "idols," yet they were absorbed into the medieval tradition. What saved them were three factors, I surmise: they were not complete bodies; they were of precious material (which had important, and positive, symbolic connotations in the Middle Ages); and they were hollow. They thus lent themselves to "conversion" by becoming containers of holy relics. I imagine the Middle Ages discarded the "bib" of the Roman busts in order to emphasize the character of the head as a fragment.[14] It was Gothic naturalism that reconstituted the shoulders and chest, thereby giving birth to a new form of bust which survived throughout the early Renaissance and far into the sixteenth century.[15]

The merging of medieval head reliquaries and Roman busts in the Quattrocento could not have occurred if early Renaissance artists had not sensed an affinity between the two.

Another such affinity links the medieval prophet and the Roman orator. It becomes evident from a comparison of two prophet statues by Donatello, made about a decade apart. The earlier one (Fig. 15), dating from about 1417, still conforms to the medieval tradition—an old man swathed in ample garments and displaying a long scroll to which he points with his right hand (Evangelists, in contrast, usually hold books). Only the head departs from the established type; instead of showing the long beard of an Eastern sage, it is cleanshaven, and obviously modeled after a Roman portrait. In the later statue (Fig. 16), the entire type has been transformed. The prophet now wears a toga that leaves one shoulder bare; his glance is directed at the beholder; and the scroll has been reduced to the size of "lecture notes" which he holds in his left hand even though he does not really need them. Apparently in the interval Donatello had come to think of Old Testament prophets as the counterpart of Roman Republican orators, those champions of moral rectitude and political freedom about whom he must have heard a great deal from his humanist friends in that age of revived classical eloquence. Did he perhaps also see images of Roman orators? What he is likely to have known are modest and small-scale figures such as that from the tomb of Quintus Sulpicius Maximus (Fig. 17), in no way comparable to his own overpoweringly expressive statue. The proof, it seems to me, is the shape of the scroll and the way it is held.[16]

To modern eyes, the Roman orator's tombstone holds little aesthetic appeal. Donatello obviously found it of greater interest, for reasons I have tried to suggest. This is one reason why the "visual philology" with which we are here concerned often resembles the hunting of the snark—our own taste, our sense of quality in the field of ancient art, is very different from that of the early Quattrocento. Nor is it only a matter of paucity of large-scale classical sculpture in those days. A great many antique works that were widely known and admired in the fifteenth century can no longer be traced today; they were lost track of during the interval, after the taste in ancient art had begun to change. A striking instance is the so-called *Bed of Policlitus,* a relief described and highly praised in Ghiberti's *Commentaries.* We know it only from Renaissance copies (Fig. 18), none of which make it easy for us to grasp what the early Renaissance saw in this piece.[17] The subject remains uncertain, perhaps because the copyists omitted some telltale attribute; all we know is what we see: a nude young woman uncovering a sleeping nude man as she sits on the edge of his bed. We may be able to share the fifteenth century's point of view a bit better once we see how Donatello has utilized the figure of the woman. She reappears in the foreground of his marble relief of the *Feast of Herod* (Fig. 19), recognizable though completely transformed. The severed head of St. John has just been brought in by a servant, and our figure shrinks away from it in horror. Her only function is to exemplify the emotional impact of the event, since she is not one of the *dramatis personae.* What must have struck Donatello in the *Bed of Policlitus* was the extraordinary twisted pose of the woman—exactly the sort of thing he had not been taught as an apprentice growing up in the Gothic workshop tradition. He wanted to use this pose, to learn from it, but he could do so only by reinterpreting it to fit the context of his own work (there was as yet no demand for amorous scenes like the *Bed of Policlitus*). That he converted a gesture of seduction into one of horror demonstrates the sovereign freedom with which he handled his classical models. If I were a psychoanalyst, I might also link this particular transformation to the artist's homosexuality. But I firmly resist this temptation.

The desire to give new dramatic impetus to traditional narrative schemes must have been one of the chief reasons for Donatello's borrowings from ancient art. Let us compare his stucco roundel showing the *Apotheosis of St. John the Evangelist* (Fig. 20) and the same scene depicted by Giotto more than a century earlier (Fig. 21). Giotto's modest stage architecture leaves us in doubt whether the scene is placed indoors or out; Donatello has developed it into a city square framed by tall buildings and seen from below, so that the upward flight of St. John achieves a wholly new, visionary quality. The city square is like an elevated stage, with a sudden drop on the side facing the beholder, and on this lower level we see a number of bystanders some of whom look up at the miraculous event. One even tries to raise himself by clinging to the edge of the stage for a better view. It is this figure that provides the clue for Donatello's source of inspiration: a Roman relief from the Arch of Constantine showing Marcus Aurelius distributing largesse (Fig. 22). The emperor does so on a tall podium, with beholders at the lower level, and here again we find the figure, seen from the back, who pulls himself up for a better view. Once again we witness Donatello's power of synthesis—only a genius could have combined this scene with a composition by Giotto and achieved so astonishing a result.[18]

And now an instance of the hunting of the snark. Donatello's *Assumption of the Virgin* (Fig. 23) shows the aged Mother of God being carried heavenward within an oval frame of clouds that is supported by angels.[19] In Orcagna's relief of the same subject, made three quarters of a century earlier and a work Donatello surely knew well, we find much the same arrangement except that the oval frame is a solid molding and that there is no angel supporting it from below (Fig. 24). It is this "bottom angel" that concerns us, for it is a new element in Donatello's composition, unknown in medieval examples. In its earliest form, our type of the Assumption shows the Virgin as a half-length figure in a small oval supported by only two flying angels (Fig. 25);[20] as the size of the oval grew, the number of angels increased to six. This formula, in turn, derives from a well-known classical model, the wreath or medallion held by flying putti, which we find on numerous Roman sarcophagi and, in Christianized form, in early medieval art (Fig. 26). Our type of the Assumption, then, developed from a composition designed for a horizontal format; hence no "bottom angel."[21] I also rather doubt that medieval art could have invented a flying angel that supports an overhead load. Well, Donatello did, and the question is, what was his source, if any? The first proposal came from an archaeologist, who pointed to a Roman sarcophagus that has been known at least since the early sixteenth century. It shows, among many other things, a group of Olympic gods seated above a bearded nude figure who emerges from behind some rocks and holds a curving veil extended over his head (Fig. 27). He represents Coelus, the personification of the sky, and the veil is the curving firmament. Could this have been Donatello's source? Maybe so, but the similarity is not really striking. The same figure, still in the role of Coelus, also appears below the enthroned Christ on early Christian sarcophagi (Fig. 28), so that Donatello might just as well have taken it from one of these.[22] For him, this too would have been a classical source, since the early Renaissance did not differentiate between ancient and early Christian art. But we note that there is no oval frame in these alleged prototypes, and that Coelus does not support anything—he merely holds a veil. These surely are significant differences. There is, however, at least one ancient work of art where Coelus actually supports an oval frame (Fig. 29).[23] The frame is inscribed with the twelve signs of the zodiac, for the months, and the figure within it personifies either the year or eternity. This seemed a rather better source for our angel. But then it struck me that in all these examples Coelus is visible only from the chest up (he is meant to emerge from behind the horizon) and that even in the last instance he does not support the oval with any show of effort, while Donatello's angel is a complete figure and labors with a considerable sense of strain. Thus a nagging doubt persisted in my mind. Donatello's angel, I felt, really looked like an Atlas supporting the world. Could Donatello possibly have seen ancient representations of Atlas in that role?

Then, some months ago, I stumbled upon the solution to my problem—in the Florentine Baptistery. Among its splendid thirteenth-century mosaics, there is one showing the dome of heaven supported by four crouching Atlas figures who are young, beardless, and evince very much the same sense of physical strain as Donatello's angel (Fig. 30). So his source in this case was not classical at all but medieval! Or at least his immediate source (needless to say, he knew the Baptistery and its mosaics like the back of his hand) ; for these medieval Atlantes are thoroughly classical in form. How did they get into the Baptistery mosaic? The artists who designed these mosaics were strongly influenced by Byzantine art, which was capable of preserving classical figure types like flies in amber, and we must assume that they imported our Atlantes along with a lot of other Byzantine artistic baggage. Yet, as supporters of the dome of heaven the Baptistery Atlantes are unique;[24] everywhere else, the dome is supported by angels, who of course show no physical effort at all but merely stand with upraised arms. Our Atlantes, then, are surrogate angels, and that must have made them particularly suitable as models for Donatello's "bottom angel."[25]

At this point we face an even more intriguing problem— what did Donatello think of the Baptistery mosaics? Did he recognize them as medieval, or did he by any chance regard them as antique? The question is less foolish than it may sound, for the early Renaissance was firmly convinced that the Baptistery (built between 1060 and 1150) was an ancient temple of Mars converted to Christian use. Thus Donatello might well have thought of the mosaics, too, as ancient; that is, he might have regarded them as dating from the time of the supposed Christianization of the Mars temple in the days of Constantine the Great. We could hardly hope for a better illustration of the circuitous ways in which the classical tradition sometimes managed to enter the early Renaissance.

I should like to conclude with a consideration of the equestrian monument of *Gattamelata* in Padua, Donatello's largest bronze work and his boldest achievement (Fig. 31). Its fame spread so rapidly that as early as 1452, a year before it was put on public view, the king of Naples wanted to engage Donatello in order to have him make a similar equestrian statue.[26] And the Venetian Republic was repeatedly twitted about permitting their general to be immortalized as if he were a conquering Caesar.[27] The fame of the monument is usually explained with the claim that it is the first bronze equestrian statue since antiquity, inspired by the *Marcus Aurelius* in Rome (Fig. 32). Actually, however, the situation is a good deal more complicated than that. First of all, the *Gattamelata* was not the first bronze equestrian statue since antiquity. The earliest recorded statues of this kind date from the late fourteenth century, some seventy-five years before the *Gattamelata;* they represented the sainted kings of Hungary and stood in front of the cathedral in Budapest until their destruction by the Turks.[28] Unfortunately, we have no adequate pictorial record of them, although they are visible, on a tiny scale, in a late-sixteenth-century view of the city. Then there was the bronze equestrian statue of Niccolò d'Este in Ferrara, commissioned of two Florentine sculptors soon after 1441, three years before Donatello received the commission for the *Gattamelata,* and unveiled in 1451, two years earlier than Donatello's statue. It was destroyed in 1796 by a revolutionary mob, and again we lack an adequate pictorial record of it.[29] Only its base, a peculiar combination of column and arch attached to the Ducal Palace in Ferrara, has survived (Fig. 33).[30] Thus, when the King of Naples needed someone to make him a bronze equestrian statue in 1452, he might have opted for the two masters of the d'Este monument in Ferrara, which after all represented a sovereign like himself and would seem a more suitable precedent than Donatello's statue of a mere general. That the king nevertheless preferred Donatello (even though he surely had seen neither monument) tells us a good deal about the importance of artistic fame in early Renaissance Italy. As for the *Marcus Aurelius* having been Donatello's source of inspiration, a single glance at the two monuments will make it obvious that they have little indeed in common. The *Marcus Aurelius* need not even have provided the idea of a bronze equestrian statue, for another Roman example was available in Italy, and in a place much nearer Padua than Rome: the so-called *Regisole* at Pavia, destroyed in the 1790's and now known to us only from some less than adequate illustrations (Fig. 34).[31] In some ways, it was closer to the *Gattamelata* than the *Marcus Aurelius,* since it had a real saddle and stirrups while the *Marcus Aurelius* had neither. The stirrups must have been added in the Middle Ages, because they were unknown in the West before the eighth century, but Donatello and his contemporaries surely accepted them as part of the original monument.[32] The "visual philology" of the *Gattamelata* is thus a rather complicated affair. As I hope to demonstrate, the statue is a synthesis of medieval and antique traditions, and I think we need to understand this in order to account for its artistic greatness and instant fame.

The *Gattamelata* was not the first bronze equestrian statue since antiquity. Nor, as we shall see, was it the first equestrian monument to a general. But it was the first *bronze* equestrian monument to a general. This fact needs explaining, for free-standing equestrian monuments, especially bronze ones, had ever since Imperial Roman times been regarded as the prerogative of the head of state and a symbol of sovereignty. The *Regisole* was not made in or for Pavia; it was the statue of a late Roman emperor which the Lombards imported from Ravenna to the new capital of their kingdom, to assert its claim as the "new Rome." Similarly, Charlemagne imported another bronze equestrian statue of a Roman emperor from Ravenna to Aachen, to show that Aachen was the "new Rome," but it caused such a scandal that it disappeared in short order. We do know of two equestrian statues of sovereigns made in the thirteenth century, but these were of stone and attached to architecture rather than free-standing.[33] The earliest free-standing equestrian statue I know of since antiquity was, until 1792, in the Cathedral of Notre Dame in Paris (the French Revolution took a heavy toll of equestrian monuments, old and new). It represented Philip the Fair, who had it erected as a thanks offering to the Virgin for his victory over the Flemish at Mons-en-Puelle in 1304. We know its appearance from several pictures and descriptions (Fig. 35).[34] How was such a statue possible, we may ask. Does it not disprove my claim that there were no free-standing statues in the Middle Ages? The head reliquaries, we recall, were a partial exception to this rule. Here, apparently, is another. What saved the equestrian statue of Philip the Fair from the odor of idolatry was that it served as a "stand-in" for the king himself offering thanks to the Madonna. Very probably it was of wood, rather than of stone or bronze, and horse and rider wore actual armor and real cloth. In other words, it was the medieval counterpart of a store dummy, a lay figure. Medieval and Renaissance churches were full of such ex-votos, until the clutter became so great that they were all taken out and destroyed.[35] It must have been northern Gothic statues like that of Philip the Fair which inspired Can Grande, the Lord of Verona, some twenty-five years later to put a stone equestrian figure of himself on top of his monumental tomb (Fig. 36). Here the Gothic equestrian statue has moved out of doors, and is certainly free-standing in the technical sense. Yet it is also the crowning ornament of a piece of architecture, like an overgrown Gothic finial; and I think it must have been this that saved it from the accusation of being an idol. Still, the statue was obviously a very presumptuous idea, designed to proclaim the sitter's megalomaniacal claims as a sovereign. (He had taken the title Can Grande so as to liken himself to the Great Khan of Cathay, the "Emperor of the East" about whose realm the most fanciful stories circulated in the West; when his tomb was opened some decades ago, the body was found wrapped in a piece of Chinese silk.) The tomb of the Can Grande set a pattern that was followed until the end of the Trecento by his local successors and by the Visconti in Milan. Only the equestrian statues of the royal saints of Hungary belong to a class we have not met otherwise in the Middle Ages, being of bronze and clearly neither tomb statues nor ex-votos. If we only knew what they looked like! I suspect, however, that they were a good deal less than lifesize, like a bronze equestrian St. George in Prague that came from the same workshop. Thus the monument to Niccolò d'Este in Ferrara, which was at least lifesize to judge from its base, was very probably the first real attempt to resume the tradition represented by the *Marcus Aurelius* and the *Regisole*.

How could a mere general such as Gattamelata, and the

general of a republic at that, claim a monument of this kind? Let us now take a quick glance at equestrian monuments to generals. They were, until the sixteenth century, an exclusively Italian tradition, as we might well expect, Italy being the land of mercenary armies and *condottieri*. Until Donatello's *Gattamelata*, however, the tradition is restricted to tombs. It begins very modestly with that of Guglielmo Berardi, who died in the battle of Campaldino in 1289. He is shown in relief on his sarcophagus, charging into battle (Fig. 37). The style is purely Gothic—it derives, in fact, from charging knights on French and English seals—but the idea may have been suggested by the tombstones of Roman mounted soldiers.[36] These Gothic equestrian tomb figures soon grew to lifesize statues, but they always remained part of a wall tomb. Many were of wood or other cheap materials and have disappeared. The earliest preserved example, made soon after 1405, is a wooden statue of very modest ambition (Fig. 38). Originally, it was probably framed by a canopy, like the slightly later tomb of Cortesia Sarego in Verona (Fig. 39), which has an equestrian statue of stone. I suspect the heirs of Gattamelata had this kind of tomb and statue in mind when they called Donatello to Padua. The idea of a bronze statue to be placed outdoors and not to be part of a tomb may well have been conceived by the artist, who "sold" it to his patrons. In fact, Gattamelata's tomb was not begun until several years after the equestrian monument had been installed; it is inside the church of St. Anthony, quite modest in scale and design, and by a minor local carver. Yet, while Donatello's statue is not part of a tomb, it is not entirely free from a funerary context. Not only does it stand in front of the church where the general is actually buried, but it stands on hallowed ground that was once the cemetery attached to that church. Moreover, the pedestal has doors in it, suggesting a burial chamber (they are, of course, not real doors, and there is no chamber behind them). We may thus term it a cenotaph, a memorial monument which is not the actual tomb. But the extraordinary fact is that such funerary symbolism as the monument has (e.g., the doors on the pedestal) is purely classical and taken from Roman sarcophagi rather than from Christian art. There is indeed no trace of Christian symbolism anywhere on the pedestal or on the statue itself. The pedestal, oval in cross-section, is termed a "columna," a column, in the documents; it is surely meant to evoke the tall columns on which ancient equestrian monuments were displayed. The *Regisole* stood on top of a column, and so did the equestrian bronze statue of Justinian in Constantinople, which was later destroyed by the Turks but which Donatello may have known about through his friend Ciriaco d'Ancona. The suggestion of a burial chamber in the base thus seems to have the purpose of keeping the monument from being too obviously "imperial." The main purpose of the statue is to serve as a monument to the general's fame, and this was clearly understood by all those who described it in the fifteenth century or composed inscriptions for it. (The monument never did receive an inscription, apparently because the Venetian government and the general's heirs could not agree on a wording.)

How did Donatello go about this novel task of creating a monument to an individual's fame? We have seen that the choice of the material, the placement outdoors, and the tall oval base evoke the memory of ancient imperial statues. But obviously Donatello could not represent the general in the guise of a Roman emperor. He had to show him as a general, and yet in such a way as to suggest more than just his individual appearance. Gattamelata had died, in advanced age and after long illness, a year before Donatello came to Padua. Even if there was a death mask or other portraits of the general, the artist could hardly make his statue a mere realistic portrait and at the same time project the aura of a hero. Needless to say, Donatello had to show Gattamelata in military costume. The kind he chose is not contemporary but armor *all'antica,* a cross between ancient and modern armor, richly embossed with figural designs that include a modified Gorgon's head on the chest (Fig. 40). The right hand holds the baton of command, the visible sign of the general's authority. None of these Roman features can be found in any ancient equestrian figures. The *Regisole* and the *Marcus Aurelius* do not wear armor, nor do they hold a baton; and the mounted officers on Roman sarcophagi or tombstones wear rather simple armor and again do not carry batons. What Donatello must have seen was a statue of a standing Roman commander such as that of Marcus Holconius Rufus (Fig. 41), which does have all the features we are looking for. Apparently he just picked it up and put it on a horse. But the resemblance of *Gatta-melata* to a Roman commander does not stop here. We can see it even in the face (Fig. 42), which despite its high degree of individuality is not a portrait in the documentary sense at all. It, too, has a distinctly Roman air, derived from ancient portrait heads (Fig. 43), a quality suggesting both intellect and *virtù*, that untranslatable word which sums up all the highest praise the Renaissance could bestow upon an individual.[37]

NOTES

1. Leonardo da Vinci, *Treatise on Painting*, A. Philip McMahon, tr. (Princeton, 1956), I, 50f.

2. On "artistic progress" and landscape painting as Renaissance phenomena, see the essays by Ernst Gombrich in his *Norm and Form* (London and New York, 1966). Pliny's discussion of the appeal of unfinished works of art is to be found in his *Natural History*, XXXV, xl, 145, 155.

3. The earliest explicit claim of this sort occurs, so far as I know, in the chronicle of Filippo Villani; cf. Julius v. Schlosser *Quellenbuch zur Kunstgeschichte des abendländischen Mittelalters [Quellenschriften*, N. F., VII] (Vienna, 1896), p. 371. For the evolution of the artist's liberal-arts status, see Rudolf and Margot Wittkower, *Born Under Saturn* (London and New York, 1963), pp. 1-16.

4. See Rudolf Wittkower, *Architectural Principles in the Age of Humanism* (London, 1949), pp. 3ff.

5. See H. W. Janson, *The Sculpture of Donatello* (Princeton, 1963), pp. 85-86.

6. Cf. John R. Spencer, "Volterra, 1466," *Art Bulletin*, XLVIII (1966), 95-96.

7. Cf. H. W. Janson, "Donatello and the Antique," *Donatello e il suo tempo, Atti dell'VIII Convegno internazionale di Studi sul Rinascimento* (Florence, 1968), pp. 77-96.

8. See Frederick Hartt and Gino Corti, *Art Bulletin*, XLIV (1962), 157, n. 12.

9. For the Avenches bust and related material see P. Schazmann, *Zeitschrift für Schweizerische Archäologie und Kunstgeschichte*, II (1940), 69ff. A recent addition to this small group, a gold bust of Antoninus Pius found at Didymoteichon, is described by A. Vavritsas, *Athens Annals of Archaeology*, I (1968), 197.

10. Suzanne Gevaert, *L'Orfévrerie Mosane au Moyen Age* (Brussels, 1943), No. 6.

11. See the technical analysis in the exhibition catalogue, *Les Trésors des Eglises de France* (Paris, Musée des Arts Décoratifs, 1965), pp. 289ff. (with bibliography).

12. Professor Irving Lavin has recently dealt with this problem in a searching paper presented at the annual meeting of the College Art Association of America in Washington, D.C., January 29-30, 1970, and now published in amplified form in *The Art Quarterly*, XXXIII (1970), 207-26.

13. Cf. Pliny's account of ancestor portraits, *Natural History*, XXXV, ii. He reports that Messala was outraged when he discovered an "alien" portrait among those of his family. Yet Pliny, to whom a portrait represents a species of immortality, suggests that false ancestry is better than no ancestry, since it betokens admiration of the virtues of the "adopted" ancestors. His remarks may help us to understand the *raison d'être* of the bust of Giovanni Chellini: in 1456, the year inscribed on the bust, Chellini established his funerary chapel and made his nephew his universal heir, all of his own children having died. Since he did not order the bust himself (had he done so, the fact would appear in his account book, which is preserved), it seems probable that the portrait was commissioned by his nephew, who through Chellini's last will had acquired considerable wealth as well as a new ancestor. If this hypothesis is correct, the nephew ordered the bust not in 1456 but after Chellini's death several years later, and the date on the bust refers not to the making of the bust but Chellini's "adoption" of his nephew as universal heir. On Chellini's account book see H. W. Janson, "Giovanni Chellini's

Libro . . . ," *Studien zur toskanischen Kunst, Festschrift für Ludwig Heinrich Heydenreich* (Munich, 1964), pp. 131ff.

14. Sainte-Foy is, to my knowledge, the only medieval reliquary representing a complete figure. The head, which is out of scale with the head, may have been kept as small as it is in order to minimize the danger of "idolatry." Two hundred years later, in the twelfth century, this fear would seem to have lessened to some degree, as evidenced by the seated funerary statues of two Carolingian kings, Louis IV and Lothaire, posthumously erected in St-Remi, Reims, and destroyed in the French Revolution. Their appearance is known from eighteenth-century engravings. The surviving fragments show that they, too, were significantly less than lifesize. See Anne Prache, *Revue de l'Art*, VI (1969), 68ff.

15. There exists in central France a group of reliquaries in the form of half-length figures (see the catalogue cited in Note 11 above, pp. 229, 236, 246) including both arms. It seems unlikely that this local type accounts for the origin of the Gothic bust reliquary. A more plausible source may be the Mosan aquamaniles in the shape of late classical busts such as the specimen in Aachen (Fig. 14); see Konrad Hoffmann, *The Year 1200* (Metropolitan Museum of Art, New York, 1970), p. 118; and H. Grundmann, "Der Cappenberger Barbarossakopf . . . ," *Münstersche Forschungen*, XII (1959), 35. So far as I know, these aquamaniles are the only medieval copies after classical busts. Significantly enough, however, they are very much smaller than lifesize (the Aachen example is 7¼" high), and they are containers.

16. See Janson, "Donatello and the Antique."

17. See Gombrich, *Norm and Form*, pp. 126, 154.

18. See Janson, "Donatello and the Antique."

19. Janson, *The Sculpture of Donatello*, pp. 88ff.

20. Mario Chiarini, *Museo Diocesano di Pistoia, Catalogo* (Florence, 1968), p. 21.

21. There is, however, a bottom angel of sorts in another type of Assumption that shows the Virgin surrounded by cherubs' heads; see Enzo Carli, *Lippo Vanni a San Leonardo al Lago* (Florence, n.d. [1969]), pl. 33.

22. See Janson, "Donatello and the Antique."

23. See M. J. Vermaseren, *The Legend of Attis in Greek and Roman Art* (Leiden, 1966), pp. 27ff., plate xvii.

24. Karl Lehmann, "The Dome of Heaven," *Art Bulletin*, XXVII (1945), 16, was able to cite only one precedent, a Roman mosaic floor in Ostia showing four standing Atlantes that support a turreted city wall. The Baptistery figures must, I believe, be regarded as reflecting the general trend toward upgrading the status of Atlantes in the thirteenth century; cf. H. W. Janson, "The Meaning of the Giganti," *Il Duomo di Milano, Congresso Internazionale . . . Atti, I* [Monografie di Arte Lombarda] (Milan, 1969), pp. 61ff. For Atlas and his transformations in early medieval manuscript illumination see Erwin Panofsky, *Studies in Iconology* (New York, 1939), pp. 20ff., figs. 7–10.

25. Mr. Jerry Draper was kind enough to draw my attention to a late Gothic "bottom angel" in a Dutch woodcut of ca. 1465 showing the Virgin and Child in Glory (Arthur M. Hind, *An Introduction to a History of Woodcut. . . .* [London, 1935], pp. 111–12); the lower half of this angel, who supports the crescent moon on which the Madonna is standing, has been lost, so that we cannot determine whether he is of the crouching, Atlas-like type.

26. See George L. Hersey, "The Arch of Alfonso . . . ," *Master Drawings*, VII (1969), 21 (two letters of Alfonso dated May 26, 1452).

27. See Janson, *The Sculpture of Donatello*, pp. 151ff.

28. See Maria G. Agghàzy, "Lasse d'Ungheria . . . ," *Il Duomo di Milano, Congresso Internazionale . . . Atti, I* [Monografie di Arte Lombarda] (Milan, 1969), pp. 89ff.

29. See Janson, *The Sculpture of Donatello*, p. 158.

30. The statue it supports today is modern.

31. Ludwig H. Heydenreich, "Marc Aurel und Regisole," *Festschrift für Erich Meyer* (Hamburg, 1959), pp. 146ff.

32. On the origin of the stirrup and its diffusion see Lynn White, Jr., *Medieval Technology and Social Change* (New York, 1962), I, ii.

33. They are the famous "Rider" in Bamberg Cathedral and Otto I in Magdeburg. See Hand Steuerwald, *Der Reitermeister . . .* , (Berlin, 1967).

34. See *Art de France*, III (1963), 127, 132.

35. Cf. Aby Warburg, *Gesammelte Schriften*, I (Glückstadt, 1933 [reprint, Nendeln, 1969]), 116ff., 349ff.

36. See the specimen reproduced in Heydenreich, "Marc Aurel und Regisole," p. 156, fig. 11.

37. See Janson, "Donatello and the Antique." For equestrian figures on medieval and Renaissance tombs, cf. Erwin Panofsky, *Tomb Sculpture* (New York, 1964), pp. 76ff.

PHOTOGRAPHIC CREDITS

A. C. L., Brussels (Fig. 10); Alinari, Florence (Figs. 2, 24, 27, 29, 30, 36, 37, 39, 41); Alinari-Anderson, Florence (Figs. 3, 28, 32); Alinari-Brogi, Florence (Figs. 1, 4, 13, 15, 42); Archives photographiques, Paris (Fig. 11); Cartovendita, Bologna (Fig. 33); Escoute, Lille (Fig. 19); Fototeca Unione, Rome (Figs. 17, 22); Gabinetto fotografico nazionale, Rome (Fig. 23); Gallerie e Musei Vaticani, Rome (Fig. 43); Hirmer, Munich (Fig. 26); Historisches Museum, Basel (Fig. 12); Münchow, Aachen (Fig. 14); Museo archeologico, Bologna (Fig. 5); Schweizerisches Landesmuseum, Zurich (Figs. 8, 9); Soprintendenza alle gallerie, Florence (Figs. 6, 20, 21, 25); Victoria and Albert Museum, London (Fig. 7).

V

Chaucer's Fifteenth-Century Successors

Norman E. Eliason
The University of North Carolina at Chapel Hill

Chaucer's successors were a luckless lot. In their attempts
to imitate him they failed, and their failure has elicited only
scorn. Instead of sympathetic consideration, which they might
seem to deserve if only because of their good judgment in
selecting Chaucer as a model, they have been roundly damned
for their inability to match him. Their language is denounced
for its excessive exuberance or prolixity and their meter casti-
gated for its irregularity. It is chiefly for these sins that literary historians have given the whole of the fifteenth century
and the first half of the sixteenth a bad name, blaming it on
"the baneful influence of Chaucer." When not dismissing
the poetry of this age with contempt, they regard it with a
none too charitable condescension.

A more judicious appraisal of these much maligned poets
has long been wanted and is now underway. In time, no doubt,
they will be seen in a more favorable light. Their eventual
fate, the merit or lack of it to be assigned them in any final
estimate, is not my concern here, however, for my interest in
the Chaucerian imitators is to see just what they thought most
worthy of imitation and just why they failed. With a clearer
understanding of the latter, we will have a clearer notion of
the former. What they especially admired in Chaucer's poetry
deserves serious notice, I think, for—whether they were right
in their judgments or not—the opinions of Chaucer's contemporaries and immediate successors may give us pause in

our own ready judgments, viewing his poetry almost six centuries later.

But though certainly not negligible, these early judgments
are not to be regarded as infallible either. Nearly all of them
occur in expressions of praise, and praise is rarely conducive
to carefully considered critcism. They are—when stripped of
matter not pertinent to us here—much too brief and scattered
to comprise anything like a comprehensive view. Moreover,
as contemporary comments often do, they exclude much which
at the time seemed perfectly obvious and therefore not worth
mentioning.

Their judgments, when due allowance is made for all this
and also for the fact that they are expressed less precisely than
we wish and are reflected rather puzzlingly in the work of
Chaucer's imitators, are very clear about one thing: in his own
day and for over a century thereafter, Chaucer was admired
primarily and almost exclusively as a poetic craftsman.[1]

Only when his craftsmanship could no longer be really
appreciated did admiration shift to other things—to Chaucer's
learning and morality, which, beginning in the first quarter of
the sixteenth century, are the main objects of praise. This
shift of attention from the manner of Chaucer's verse to its
matter, where it was long to rest and in recent years has been
vigorously renewed, has tended to belittle the judgment of
his early admirers.

Lydgate, who acknowledged Chaucer as his master, called
him "the firste fyndere of our faire langage," and Hoccleve,
who also acknowledged him as master, said that Chaucer was
the "firste to distille and reyne / The golde dewe droppis of
speche and eloquence / In-to oure tounge thourg his excellence / And founde the flourys first of rethoryk / Our rude
speche oonly to enlumyne." Comments like this, which are
repeated throughout the century, seem to suggest that their
admiration for Chaucer's craftsmanship was confined solely to
his language and did not extend to his versification. That
they had both in mind, however, is indicated by the fact that
it is as a poet, not simply a writer, that they praised him, and

the extravagance of their praise suggests that it was elicited by his "fayre makyng" rather than only by his "faire langage." Their admiration of his versification is certainly less clear than that of his language, about which their comments are fairly lucid and their judgments sound. It is these which we shall consider first and then return to their views about versification.

The qualities of Chaucer's language which were especially admired in the fifteenth and early sixteenth century are, I believe, its aptness, freshness, conciseness, and polish. This is quite different from Miss Spurgeon's view, for she characterizes them as *"golden tonged, eloquent, 'ornate'."*[2] As a rubric this may do well enough perhaps, but unfortunately her brief discussion of the matter is equally vague and uncritical and places undue emphasis upon ornateness and what she calls Chaucer's "rhetorical powers"—two qualities which I regard with considerable skepticism.

That Chaucer's fifteenth-century admirers regarded his language as ornate and praised it as such is quite true.[3] What they really meant, however, is uncertain. To them, aware as they were or professed to be of the "rudeness" of the language of Chaucer's predecessors and contemporaries, his language no doubt seemed so much more refined that the term *ornate* seemed appropriate. If, as seems likely, it was in this comparative sense that they used the term, it would be interesting to know precisely which poetry they thought of as being less ornate or more "rude"—whether the more popular poetry of the time, such as romances or ballads, or that of Chaucer's contemporaries, Langland and the *Gawain* poet, neither of whom Chaucer's admirers mention but whom they would probably have regarded as "rude" too.

Lydgate's characterization of Chaucer as "noble rethor," echoed repeatedly in one way or other by his later admirers throughout the century also poses a semantic problem, but of a different kind. Whether the term, bestowed in and meant as praise, really signified "rhetorician" or simply "good writer" is, I think, questionable. It is usually construed in the former sense with the explanation[4] that the term is properly applicable as evidenced by his knowledge of rhetoric and the wide use he made of it in his poetry. For reasons that I shall not go into here, the demonstration seems to me unconvincing. All that needs mention here, where our concern is the validity of fifteenth century judgment of Chaucer as a rhetorician,[5] is that *rhetoric* is thus taken as referring to the discipline rather than the art, to the body of rules formulated in treatises of the late Middle Ages rather than the things such rules were concerned with—effective expression and the means of achieving it. This, I believe, is a fallacy.[6] There is no reason for assuming that the fifteenth-century admirers of Chaucer's rhetoric had in mind only the technical sense of the term and not at all its more general and more basic sense. If so, they had better judgment than most commentators about Chaucer's rhetoric today, who insist upon shrinking its meaning to the rather trivial aspects of rhetoric singled out for attention in the medieval treatises on the subject and neglect its more fundamental and vital aspects, such as structure, style, and tone—aspects which Chaucer gave heed to and which, I believe, his fifteenth-century admirers appreciated even though they did not fully apprehend them. In believing this, I am crediting them merely with good common sense, not with any remarkable powers of critical acumen.

Turning now to the qualities of Chaucer's language mentioned earlier, let us first briefly examine the evidence indicating that they were in fact the ones that were admired and then consider some of the implications of this. The terms which I apply to them are modern and not simply the ones employed by the fifteenth- and early sixteenth-century commentators. Relying exclusively on their terms leads only to confusion or distortion.[7]

Aptness was not yet in use in the fifteenth century to describe language, but "aptness" or some meaning very much like it was clearly what the commentators had in mind. Few are quite as explicit about it, however, as the anonymous author of *The Book of Curtesye* (1473) who, after praising Chaucer's language for being "clear in sentence," and written "briefly," adds, "His langage was so fayr and pertynente / It semeth vnto mannes heerynge / Not only the worde but verely the thynge." Less explicitly concerned with aptness, perhaps, but significant as a pointed observation about Chaucer's clarity of language in this comment of Skelton (1507):

> His tearmes were not darcke,
> But pleasaunt, easy, and playne;
> No worde he wrote in vayne.

Freshness is a term used in a number of the comments—for example, Skelton's praise (1523) of Chaucer because he "Our englysshe rude so fresshely hath set out" and George Ashby's characterization of him, Gower, and Lydgate as the "firste finders . . . off freshe, douce englisshe." None however explains it in any detail. It is fairly obvious, however, that they were referring mainly to two things—Chaucer's avoidance of trite and traditional poetic diction, including the rime-tags and formulas cluttering up the "rude" English poetry which they deplored, and his ability to infuse a new vitality or liveliness into his language. The latter is evident in Lydgate's disparagement (1401) of his own language as "dull & blont" in comparison with the "gay style" of Chaucer, and in Skelton's praise (1523) of him as the one "who nobly enterprysed/ How that our englysshe myght fresshely be ameude [i.e., *amoved,* 'stirred up']."

Chaucer's conciseness is extolled by several commentators, who make their meaning quite plain—for example Caxton (ca. 1483), who says that Chaucer "wrytteth no voyde wordes but alle his mater is ful of hye and quycke sentence" and the author of *The Book of Curtesye,* who commends him for "eschewyng prolyxyte" and "castyng away the chaf of super-fluyte."

Polish, like *freshness,* is a term repeatedly applied to Chaucer's language but without any clear indication of what was really meant. Skelton, who I think really admired only its other qualities, nevertheless expresses approval (1523) of its "pullisshyd eloquence." But he was, I believe, using the term more in its negative than in its positive sense and was referring to Chaucer's ability to avoid crudity of expression rather than to achieve smoothness or elegance there. The notion that Chaucer had refashioned a language free from all its former barbarousness is expressed again and again. Lydgate says (1426) that Chaucer was "the ffyrste in any age / That amendede our langage" and later adds (1430) that he "did his besynesse . . . Out of our tounge tauoyden al Rudnesse / And to Reffourme it with Colours of swetnesse." Shirley (ca. 1456) calls Chaucer the "moste famous poete þat euer was tofore him as in þemvelisshing of oure rude moders englisshe tonge." Their mention of sweetness and embellishment reveals their awareness that the polish of Chaucer's language involved something more than merely the avoidance of crudity. Its casual elegance contrived with such apparent ease probably eluded them, just as it frequently eludes us still.

Further evidence of admiration for these qualities of aptness, freshness, conciseness, and polish is to be found in the work of Chaucer's imitators, where it is easy to overlook, however, for quite naturally it is obscured. Thus Lydgate, for example, who admired the polish of Chaucer's language, achieved a comparable polish but at the expense of aptness and with total loss of freshness. He managed very well to avoid all "rudeness" by resorting to stereotyped phraseology, apparently not realizing that a phrase, however apt it may once have been, ceases to be apt when repeated again and again and that a fresh phrase when overworked becomes a dull cliché.

Lydgate thus provides an instructive example of how a Chaucerian imitator, by neglecting one quality of Chaucer's language in favor of another, might seem to fail completely. This kind of thing is a common failing of imitators in all ages and is readily understandable. And accordingly Lydgate's language, though usually dismissed as a poor imitation of Chaucer's—as indeed it is—is not a matter that scholars have fretted over, as they have over the language of some of Chaucer's later imitators like Hawes or Skelton.

Yet the failure of these latter two is comparable to Lydgate's, though with one obvious difference, for what they did—each in his own way and with strikingly unlike results—was to single out the quality of Chaucer's language each admired most and then try to emulate rather than imitate it. In their emulation they strove not simply to equal Chaucer but to outdo him. The result was not a poor imitation but rather a distortion of Chaucer's language.

Hawes evidently admired Chaucer's diction particularly, which he praised (1503–4) for its "eloquent terms subtle and couert" (i.e., *covert,* "obscure, not plain"). Just why he praised it thus is hard to say. What he must have had in mind was about the same thing that those had who praised it as ornate or polished. What he did however is perfectly clear, for he proceeded to embellish his language with terms far more eloquent, subtle, and covert than Chaucer's, believing or wanting to believe that in this respect he could excel his master. To the polished language of Chaucer he added the gaudy glitter of his own aureate terms, for which he has earned the bemused blame of both those who have sought to explain why Hawes and others like him managed to imitate Chaucer so badly and those who have tried to account for the seemingly inexplicable vogue of aureate diction in this period.

Skelton seems to have admired Chaucer's language for its aptness, conciseness, and polish. Unlike Hawes, who found Chaucer's terms subtle and covert, he found them easy and plain, and scoffs (1507) at those who, like Hawes, sought to improve on Chaucer's language by embellishing it:

> And now men wold have amended
> his [Chaucer's] english, where at they barke
> And marre all they warke.

But Skelton then proceeds to amend Chaucer's English even more drastically than any of the aureate embellishers by his striving to be more succinct and plain-spoken than Chaucer and succeeds in marring his work by an extravagantly boisterous diction which Chaucer would have scoffed at for its "newe-fangelnesse."

If the imitators of Chaucer's language missed the mark, aiming too low, like Lydgate, or too high, like Hawes and Skelton, they deserve some credit for trying, for recognizing what the mark really was and that it was worth aiming at. The imitation of language is bound to fail when it spans a century or more of time, for with the passage of time taste changes and so too does language. By the beginning of the sixteenth century, Chaucer's language was no longer really imitable. Any attempt at faithful imitation could lead only to quaint archaism, as Spenser was to demonstrate. The best that any-one who really looked to Chaucer as his master in language could hope to find there was a model for comparable aptness, conciseness, freshness, and polish. His imitators, from the earliest on down, furnish proof of this—if proof of anything so obvious is needed. Their very failure underscores the fact that they admired Chaucer's language and thought it possessed certain qualities which they deemed significant.

These qualities as I have designated them are general, to be sure, and may therefore seem not very remarkable. They are the only ones for which I can find any clear evidence of high esteem and almost the only ones even mentioned by his successors. This is regrettable perhaps, but not really sur-prising. One might wish that Chaucer's fifteenth- and six-teenth-century admirers had been enterprising or discerning enough to mention some more specific aspects of his language which today attract notice. They say nothing about its phon-ology, grammar, or vocabulary. One could not expect any systematic treatment of the phonology, of course, but it would be interesting to find some remark or other about the sound of Chaucerian English as apprehended fifty or a hundred years later. Much the same is true about the grammar, where one might reasonably expect some mention of certain forms or constructions that must have seemed rather odd or puzzling by the early sixteenth century. Regarding vocabulary, any of Chaucer's successors might well have made an interesting observation about the words he thought peculiar to Chaucer or about some of Chaucer's vulgar or frank terms or about his French borrowings. That Chaucer uses many words of French origin is a matter passed over in either silence or perhaps indifference, and so too are other manifestations of French influence on his language—style, for example. Chaucer's style elicits only the one observation, that it is gay. The dialect in which Chaucer wrote, that of his native London, is unmentioned, even by his Scottish admirers, who might have had something interesting to say about it. His use of dialect as a literary device, in which he was a pioneer, attracts no notice at all. There is little point in extending the list of unmentioned possibilities any further. The fact that so many specific aspects of language are ignored might suggest that these writers were neither careful readers of Chaucer nor observant of such aspects of language. But this is not the case. Their comments reveal close familiarity with Chaucer and the fact that they too were writers means that they were very much concerned with precisely the kinds of things which I have mentioned.

One minor specificity which I have not mentioned before but which does receive their notice is Chaucer's use of proverbs. Lydgate (1420) praises him for the "many proverbe divers and unkouth" and the "sawes swete" in his "crafty writinge"; and John Metham (1448–9) declares that "proffoundely / With many proverbys hys bokys be rymyd naturelly." Their point evidently is not simply that Chaucer used proverbs copiously but that he used them effectively.

The admiration for Chaucer's language in the fifteenth and early sixteenth centuries as apt, concise, clear, and polished is neither perfunctory, uninformed, nor traditional. Their praise is much too enthusiastic to be anything but genuine. Their admiration of these particular qualities is inspired only by the fact that they found them present in Chaucer's poetry and lacking in his predecessors'. It is a practical judgment deriving from first-hand experience, not a theoretical judgment deriving from treatises on rhetoric. These were the qualities which they themselves found and admired in Chaucer's language.

That in their admiration for Chaucer's craftsmanship they had in mind his versification as well is certainly far from obvious if one depends solely on their comments, which rarely mention versification at all and almost never in any revealing way. The fact that the favorite verse forms of the fifteenth and early sixteenth centuries were rime-royal and the five-stress couplet, verse forms which Chaucer established and which were his favorites too, surely indicates appreciation of some sort. But precisely what aspects of his versification they really appreciated or fully comprehended is hard to say in view of their notorious lack of success in matching it.

Their failure to match the felicity of Chaucer's versification is not surprising, for few English poets ever have been able to. But their failure to match its simplest element, the meter, and its most conspicuous trait, its regularity, is something of a puzzle. The metrical irregularity of Chaucer's English imitators, beginning with his contemporaries, Hoccleve and Lydgate, and continuing well into the sixteenth century is usually attributed to the ineptness of these poets or, more particularly, to their insensibility to rhythm.[8] The latter is simply incredible. Granted that they were not the poetic equals of Chaucer, that their ears were not as finely tuned as his to the delicate effects achievable in versification, still they must have been capable of at least the metrical competence displayed by untutored ballad makers of the era. Metrical regularity is a small achievement, requiring nothing more remarkable than the ability to keep time, tapping it out if necessary with one's foot. Unless we are to assume that the fifteenth century is unique in its lack of this small accomplishment, that only then was the poetic muse too slew-footed for this, we must seek a more reasonable explanation.

Two things account for this metrical irregularity, I believe—the change which occurred in the language so that, as the century advanced, Chaucer's meter could not be understood aright, and the misconception of his meter, which was slight enough at first but grew greater with the passage of time. Before turning to these specific things, a more general consideration that may well have entered in is worth brief notice.

Whether those who admired Chaucer's craftsmanship realized that it involved not simply his language or versification but the way he managed to combine the two is not completely clear. At any rate, I have found no explicit statement about it.[9] His admirers, however, could hardly have failed to be impressed by his remarkable success in reconciling the infinitely varied patterns of normal speech with the simple and rigid patterns of meter. Dazzled by this or confounded by it, they may have felt that the combination was beyond their powers and that it was better for them to try to emulate only one or the other. Just as they went astray in their quest of language as good as Chaucer's or even better by concentrating on one particular quality to the neglect of another, the same exuberant quest may have led to the neglect of versification or to what they considered an improvement upon it. The extreme metrical irregularity of some of his later followers, like Skelton or Wyatt, is obviously not unintentional. Such meter, they must have felt, was somehow good in itself or somehow enhanced the language, making it seem more fresh, apt, or concise than was possible under the constraints of regular meter.

Chaucer's meter was not fully comprehended even by his contemporaries, Hoccleve and Lydgate. Commonly described now either as iambic pentameter (or tetrameter) or as decasyllabic (or octosyllablic), Chaucer's meter is best described, I believe, as a line of five (or four) stresses falling on alternate syllables. This meter is Chaucer's own—differing from Gower's, which is iambic tetrameter, and from Hoccleve's, which is decasyllabic—and it is his one contribution to English metrics, for it was he who consciously contrived it, I think, and only he who managed to adhere to it very carefully. Lydgate, alone among his contemporaries apparently, perceived the singularity of Chaucer's meter and tried to imitate it,[10] going wrong mainly because he could or would not adhere to it strictly.

Among Chaucer's later imitators, I doubt that any understood his meter aright. Most of them probably construed the varying length of his lines (nine to eleven syllables, as his meter allowed) and his apparently indiscriminate shifting from iamb to trochee or *vice versa* (again as his meter allowed) as license for metrical irregularity. Once his imitators believed that metrical irregularity was warranted by their model, they extended the practice more and more, so that by the end of the century, Chaucer's meter could not be appreciated at all.

Hastening this development and contributing to it were the changes taking place in the language, one of which—the loss of *e* in a final unstressed syllable—was peculiarly inimical to preserving Chaucer's meter intact.[11] This *e*, which is essential to Chaucer's meter, is not something which he added or omitted simply as the meter required. It was as genuine as any other sound in the language spoken in Chaucer's day, and its use was therefore perfectly legitimate. So too was its omission, for Chaucer omitted it regularly only when there was proper sanction—a sanction provided by the long-established poetic convention of eliding *e* in certain phonetic contexts[12] and by the existence of variant forms with *e* and without it.

This *e*, genuine as it was, nevertheless had a precarious status, for in London speech of the time, it was on its way out. The upper class, I am inclined to think, or at any rate, old-fashioned speakers, still pronounced it, but the lower class, or those who "leet olde thynges pace," dropped it. This posed a problem for Chaucer, who, instead of vacillating between the two fashions, chose the older one as the basis for his verse.

His choice may conceivably have been determined by his personal distaste for "newefangelnesse" or by the traditional poetic preference for language that was old rather than new. It is far more likely, and in my opinion virtually a certainty, that his decision was a conscious and deliberate one. It was also a very canny one, providing him with a metrically useful *e*, which he could ignore, however, when circumstances warranted.[13] The opportunity to exploit *e* in this way would have been denied him if he had chosen the *e*-less type for his verse, for when an *e* was metrically desirable he would have had to do without it or to add it in defiance of linguistic propriety.

Chaucer's canniness in relying on this obsolescent *e* and his cunning exploitation of it were evidently appreciated by Gower, who follows the same practice of keeping *e* and avoiding it as the meter requires, but were lost on Hoccleve and Lydgate. They were a generation younger than Chaucer and Gower, and to them this *e* must have seemed archaic. Instead of a sound still current in London speech, though only among a diminishing number, it had become passé. They were puzzled, I think, about whether they ought to use it at all, but to imitate Chaucer's meter, as they tried hard to do, they were forced to do so. Their failure to use it consistently and to avoid it skillfully reflects this uncertainty.[14] Their rather helter-skelter employment of *e*[15] certainly shows that it proved a hindrance rather than a help to their meter.

The distinction I have drawn between final *e* as being obsolescent in Chaucer's day and archaic a generation later is a fine one, to be sure, and my reliance on the distinction to explain the skillful use of *e* by Chaucer and Gower, on the one hand, and its fumbling use by Hoccleve and Lydgate, on the other, may seem questionable. It accords with the facts, however, as best linguists have been able to determine them, departing from their views only by being more precise about three matters: (1) the date when final *e* was generally lost in London speech and accordingly became obsolescent, which by my reckoning would be about 1350, or when Chaucer was still a boy, and also the date when it was no longer pronounced even by the elderly and accordingly became archaic, which would be ca. 1390, or when Hoccleve and Lydgate were still boys; (2) the speech-level where the loss began, which almost certainly was colloquial or lower class; and (3) the reason for the persistence of *e* in poetry, which I would attribute squarely to metrical exigency.[16] My confidence about these matters is more apparent than real, for further investigation is needed. My conclusions derive primarily from the metrical practices of the time and from my conviction that the metrical fumbling of Chaucer's immediate followers needs to be viewed not simply as a mark of their poetic ineptitude but also as a means of determining the reasons for the metrical doubts and difficulties confronting these writers.

If Chaucer's *e* was puzzling to his immediate followers and proved a vexation in their efforts to imitate him, it completely baffled his later followers and frustrated any of their real attempts at imitation of his meter. When not led astray by the usage of Lydgate, whom they often confused or bracketed with Chaucer, or by erroneous *e*'s in the Chaucer texts at their disposal, they still could not make out what Chaucer's *e* represented. They knew of course that *e* had once been pronounced and that in Chaucer it was evidently to be pronounced too sometimes, but they had no means of ascertaining when or why. An *e* in a final unstressed syllable, so far as they could tell, was one of many quaint Chaucerian usages. When imitating his meter, they either ignored his *e* or added one willy-nilly—a purely fake *e*.

In Scotland, his imitators fared better with meter because they were neither puzzled nor baffled by his *e*. In the North, *e* was lost a century earlier than in London, so that by the time of Henryson, Dunbar, and Douglas the Chaucerian *e* was no longer usable there. The only course open to them was to establish a meter not dependent on this *e*. And this is what they did, fashioning out of the language currently spoken there a new kind of verse, comparable to Chaucer's in its meter but not a slavish imitation or a bastard distortion of it.

If they could do this, it may be asked, why couldn't the poets in the South do so too? The answer, I think, is that among the English poets memory of *e* lingered on, however fuzzily, tempting them to use it when it was no longer really usable, and because enough time had not yet elapsed for them to learn how to compensate for its loss. This was not a simple matter, for it required the development of a new poetic idiom and of facility in using it. In the North this took about 250 years,[17] and in the South about the same length of time.[18] Nor is it surprising that it took so long, for the syllabic re-structuring of the language[19] meant that new means of achiev-ing meter had to be devised—a task as difficult as that faced by earlier poets in giving up the old alliterative meter in favor of the new meter, which Chaucer was the first to use with success but which his predecessors had trouble with.[20]

Meter and rime, the basic elements of versification and the only ones I am considering here, are equally subject to the ravages of linguistic change. Meter, as we have seen, suffered because of change in unstressed vowels. Rime did not, despite the fact that stressed vowels underwent radical change during the same period. Stressed vowels, however, were not elim-inated; they were merely pronounced differently. The poets of the fifteenth and early sixteenth centuries had no more trouble with riming than he did, and their riming like his was usually true. This was not due directly to the influence of Chaucer, for many of his rimes must have seemed false by the end of the fifteenth century. It is due rather to a poetic convention, antedating Chaucer but greatly strengthened by his example of avoiding false rimes of any kind—a convention which was not abandoned until the eighteenth century.[21] Con-cerning Chaucer's rimes, which are noteworthy as being even more regular than his meter, his followers have significantly nothing to tell us.

This brief and superficial survey of Chaucer's successors will have served a useful purpose if it does nothing more than remind us of what we have known all along, or at least since the publication of Miss Spurgeon's work over a generation ago, that it was Chaucer's poetic craftsmanship that most im-pressed his early admirers. This view is much too sound to be dismissed as naive or quaint. His craftsmanship proved un-matchable, as his imitators were to discover in time and to their own discomfiture. Their failure, usually denounced as mere ineptitude, merits more sympathetic and thoughtful consideration than it has had, if only because of what it reveals

1. This conclusion is essentially the same as Caroline Spurgeon's, though she states it in different terms. *Five Hundred Years of Chaucer Criticism and Allusion* (Cambridge, 1925), I, xciii f.

I have relied heavily on her work, of course, and have taken almost all my citations from it.

2. *Ibid.*, p. xciii.

3. Thus, for example, King James I of Scotland praises Chaucer together with Gower for their "eloquence ornate"; in *The Book of Curtesye* Chaucer is apostrophized as the "fader and founder of ornate eloquence"; and Caxton similarly calls him "the worshipful fader & first founder & embelissher of ornate eloquence in our englissh."

4. E.g., by Jerome Mitchell, "Hoccleve's Tribute to Chaucer," in *Chaucer und seine Zeit* (Tübingen, 1968), pp. 282–83.

5. But equally applicable to modern judgments about it too.

6. A common error with words like *grammar, rhetoric,* etc., referring both to a formulated system (e.g., transformational *grammar, rhetoric* of fiction) and to the phenomena which the system attempts to account for (e.g., the *grammar* of English). *Rhetoric,* from the fourteenth century and on, refers to both—cf. *OED* definition 1 *vs.* definitions 2 and 3.

7. As is true of Miss Spurgeon's account, noted above.

8. The case is stated with vigor by Eleanor Hammond, *English Verse between Chaucer and Surrey* (Duke University Press, 1927), who repeats the charge again and again, sometimes varying it a bit but without essential modification.

9. The closest to such a comment is Lydgate's remark about his own verse and his fear that it is not up to the standard of Chaucer:

> Alway with feare betwyxt drede and shame
> Leste oute of lose, any word asterte
> In this metre, to make it seme lame,
> Chaucer is deed that hade suche a name
> Of fayre makyng that [was] without wene
> Fayrest in our tonge . . .
> We may assay forto countrefete
> His gay style but it wyl not be.

At any rate, Lydgate seems aware that in the 'fayre makyng' of his master, meter as well as language was an important element.

10. Hence his many headless lines, erroneously censured by modern critics who seem to overlook them in Chaucer. Lydgate's broken back lines (i.e., lines lacking an unstressed syllable at the caesura) are evidently modeled on Chaucer, who, though adding an extra unstressed syllable at the caesura occasionally, omits the unstressed syllable there only rarely. The latter apparently caught Lydgate's fancy, and he proceeded to omit the syllable there often enough so that it is known now as the "Lydgate line." This explanation is essentially the same as that of Derek Pearsall in *Chaucer and Chaucerians,* ed. D. S. Brewer (London, 1967),p. 206.

11. Obviously this is not the only change affecting his meter, nor is the loss of *e* as simple a matter as I seem to regard it here. This is not the place to consider either its complexities or any of the other changes. Our

Norman E. Eliason

special concern is the regularity of Chaucer's meter, which depends—though not exclusively—on the pronunciation of *e*. It is therefore of crucial significance.

12. Usually described merely as prevocalic, which, I think, is inadequate, for Chaucer uses elision with more latitude than this.

13. Any latitude he allowed himself about this would not have seemed odd, for it was in line with the current speech trend. It is inconceivable that Chaucer was unaware of the fact that final *e* was disappearing.

14. Pearsall's view (*Chaucer and Chaucerians*, pp. 205–6) seems to be at complete odds with mine, but I doubt that it really is. I think he construes Chaucer's meter too loosely and therefore errs in thinking that Lydgate "uses final -*e* under much the same conditions as Chaucer, except in his [Lydgate's] later works" (p. 205). He describes Hoccleve's meter as "even and regular, though with an over-careful attention to the syllable count which often results in wrenched stress" (p. 224). He might well have added that in counting his syllables Hoccleve included and omitted final *e* in a way that would have appalled Chaucer.

15. Scribal inaccuracy is not to blame alone, nor are Lydgate and Hoccleve the only fifteenth-century poets to suffer because of bad texts. Sorting out authentic and erroneous *e*'s there is a hopeless task. It is difficult enough in Chaucer, where metrical regularity provides some guidance.

16. Linguists usually date the loss as fourteenth century, shying off from anything more precise or early mainly because of the Chaucerian evidence. Though often implying that it was a colloquial development, they are not at all explicit about it. They apparently see no connection between this and the fact that *e* is preserved in verse, which they either view with suspicion or describe simply as an archaism. (See J. W. and E. M. Wright, *An Elementary Middle English Grammar* [1934], ¶142; Jordan-Matthes, *Handbuch der Mittelenglischen Grammatik* [1934], ¶s 141 and 290; K. Luick, *Historische Grammatik der englischen Sprache* [1921], ¶473.) E. Talbot Donaldson (*PMLA*, LXIII (1948), 1101–30) comes closest to my view in general, I think, and certainly to my belief that *e* was obsolescent in Chaucer's day: "Chaucer may have survived the final -*e* in the London area by some years, or, less probably, it may have survived him by a few: we do not know" (p. 1111). [To which, from *or* on, I would demur.] Forms with final *e*, he adds, "whether or not they were still used by the Court and the people of London, had probably been used by Chaucer's father, and had the sanction of all previous South English literature, including Gower" (p. 1115).

17. I.e., from the time when final *e* was lost there (before 1250) to the time of Henryson, Dunbar, and Douglas. James I precedes them, and it is interesting to note that in *The Kingis Quaire e* is sometimes retained. It is now believed that the language of the poem was originally Southern English but was later altered by Scottish scribes.

18. I.e., from 1350, when final *e* ceased to be pronounced in colloquial London speech, to the time of the sixteenth-century sonneteers, who restore metrical regularity.

19. Involving not only the loss of final unstressed syllables and medial syllables but also changes in word-stress. I know of no study of the metrical effect of this restructuring and of the means devised to offset it.

20. It took them about 250 years too, i.e., from the time of the last really good Old English poem (*Maldon*, 991) to the first really good Middle English poem (*The Owl and the Nightingale*, ca. 1200)—a comment which, I trust, will not be taken in dead earnest, nor combined with the comments in notes

17 and 18 to suggest that I am trying to set up "metrochronology" as a new science.

21. The point is well made by H. C. Wyld in his *Studies in English Rhymes from Surrey to Pope* (London, 1923). He might just as well have used Chaucer as his starting point, but evidently did not because he wanted to buttress his argument by citing orthoepistic evidence, lacking before the sixteenth century.

ˌ

VI

Cinquecento Mannerism
and the
Uses of Petrarch

Aldo Scaglione
The University of North Carolina at Chapel Hill

Beauté, mon beau souci, de qui l'âme incertaine,
a comme l'Océan son flux et son reflux.

(Malherbe)

When De Sanctis began to canvass his sweeping indictment of the Italian Cinquecento by focusing his strictures upon the work of Ariosto and Guicciardini, he was bringing to ultimate fruition the basic preoccupation of the man of the Risorgimento—of whom he made himself the literary standard-bearer—with the social significance of all culture.[1] Coherent as it still appears to us in the depths of its moral motivations, that judgment was visibly unfair. De Sanctis was bringing forth charges of formalism and scepticism, and we know now that the works at stake were representing, rather, an abstract and relativistic orientation, this being not a sign of decay but of a new vitality and creative opening toward future developments of great import for all of European culture.

This realization on our part is aided by a new understanding of the deep texture of Cinquecento literature in the light of a recent critical discovery, namely what art historians have come to call Mannerism.

The reinterpretation of portions of the Italian Cinquecento through the concept of Mannerism seems to me one of the more engaging endeavors in current literary studies. This

[122]

reassessment, long overdue in the eyes of some art historians, and now apparently underway in the laboratories of the literary historians, is of direct concern to all students of the European sixteenth and seventeenth centuries. The matter is still fresh and highly problematic. I shall spare you the details of this controversy.[2] Suffice it to say that many a caveat must be entered in any such quest. We must resist the temptation to overexpand the value of a periodic concept beyond that of a cultural common denominator, lest it become a dogmatic schema which looses specific meaning by wanting to cover too much.[3] We must also keep clearly in mind that art history and literary history necessarily show analogies, yet follow each their own tracks. Thus our definition of the term will have to be meaningful to the art historian and yet take account of the autonomy of every discipline, so that while we avoid judging an activity with criteria which belong to another, we nevertheless describe general relationships through categories which acquire a specific and appropriate context within the area they invest.[4] More important still, we must be aware of the rich variety of trends and personalities in the century in question; thus any indication of collective orientation, such as that implied by the term Mannerism, not only cannot affect all the literature of the period, but may not even serve to cover all the production of a single personality, or reach all its essential aspects. This demurrer is especially timely in the case of, say, an Ariosto, who, we may be prepared to admit, does contain some notable Manneristic traits, but is not a Mannerist in a central way. And how could he be, since the *Furioso* (first completed in 1516) antedates even the earliest clearly recognizable works of Mannerist painting and it is widely accepted that Mannerism started out in painting and radiated from there through the other arts and art theory with varying time lags of up to half a century?

At the other end of the century, Tasso comes very near to closing the parabola of the Mannerist experience (unless one should choose, as some do, to deny Marino to the Baroque in order to assign him to a late Mannerism, in the very respectable

and quite plausible company of his quasi-contemporaries Gón-
gora, Shakespeare, and Cervantes) .[5] This view of his exquisite
achievement should end once and for all—if this were possible—
the prolonged debates on whether he was Baroque, pre-Baroque, or late Renaissance. The most sensitive critics seem to
be coming around to this new perspective of Tasso as the last
great Mannerist. And this is far more than a matter of idle
labels. As Raimondi has shrewdly pointed out, in speaking of
the otherwise admirable study of Tasso by the late Ulrich Leo,
it is "in effect absurd" to speak of the poet of the *Liberata*
as the forerunner of Baroque because we are at the same time
compelled, in a glaring logical contradiction, to stress that
neither was his mind Baroque nor his style *concettista,* so that
he would be sharing responsibility for something with which
he had nothing directly in common.[6]

But since our present concern lies chiefly with the Cinquecento lyric, we may content ourselves with a few brief observations on the aspects of Ariosto and Tasso that might be regarded as related to Mannerism. In his neofeudal, neogothic
revival of the popular medieval knights Boiardo had introduced
a peculiar treatment of chivalrous heroes virtually abstracted
from any recognizable social reality, as denizens of a world of
pure artistic fiction which I have elsewhere called "idyllic"
because of its carefree, elegantly stylized absorption into a
dreamlike atmosphere where all moral assessments tend to
become definitively suspended and de facto irrelevant.[7] Ariosto
carried this process to its extreme consequences, even to the
extent of further dissolving, as it were, the individual traits of
both Boiardo's characters and their locales, so as to homogenize
them as the uniform beings and places of an abstract world that
has no point of contact with any other reality than that of the
poet's subjective creation. The poet creates his world, peoples
it with his own creatures, and moves the latter about on the
basis of his own, newly set laws and rules. The resulting effect
is that of a cosmos in which everything, every pattern of behavior seems nonsensical and absurd from close view (since it
responds to none of our moral imperatives), whereas it fits

into a special order (like that of a god's creation) only when seen from a distance, as a whole. And yet, this supremely polished and apparently serene, nay Olympian representation seems to carry a somewhat hidden, discreetly yet powerfully stated message that unexpectedly reconnects that idyl to our world, with a resultant disquieting jolt to the reader. For in terms of emotional impact on the reader the main hero of the poem is not Orlando but the tragic, impiously sublime Rodomonte. This arch-individualist who fights more for his own pride than for any organized cause fills more books than any other with his presence; and it is, after all, with his horrible death that the poem itself closes—when, his forehead horribly split by Ruggiero's dagger, his soul departs to take her due place in Hell, not without casting one final curse on Gods and men: "bestemmiando fuggì l'alma sdegnosa, / che fu sì altiera al mondo e sì orgogliosa." Rodomonte's whole story stands out as the most intriguing, the most puzzling, the most "human" in the poem. Having lost his fickle fiancée to Mandricardo and having thus concluded once for all, through the additional confirmation of the innkeeper's Giocondo story (Canto 28), that there is no faith or virtue in women anywhere and anytime, having thus embarked upon a self-proclaimed career as unbending woman-hater, Rodomonte then becomes, with a reversal as dramatic as it is sudden, the defender of unparalleled womanly virtue before the whole world. The change of heart is brought about by the discovery of Isabella's matchless faithfulness to Zerbino when, rather than bending to Rodomonte's desires, she causes him to behead her, alas!, quite unintentionally, through the stratagem of the magic infusion, her chosen form of martyrdom. This paradoxical and, in its deep irony, tragic story unconsciously induces the reader into a mood of disturbed acceptance of the poet's deep message: for the world represented by Ariosto is, to say it with Croce's formula, one of "cosmic harmony"; but the stuff of which this harmonious cosmos is made is nothing less than chaos—moral and social chaos.[8] The Italian wars, the incipient religious crisis, and the crumbling of the liberal political hopes under the onslaught of the new despotisms were causing second thoughts on the validity of the humanistic hopes as to man's perfectibility and nobility. Ariosto was mirroring such troubled conditions through the distorted psyches and the individualistic, nay egotistic drifting of the knights into webs of insoluble conflicts. It is particularly this achievement which places him alongside some masters of Mannerist art. The reader is artistically provoked by Rodomonte's horrid enormities just as is the spectator by the falling giants in Giulio Romano's Palazzo del Té or, in a different way, by the monsters of Bomarzo—so unnatural and yet so human.[9] Tasso's contacts with Mannerism should be more obvious still; therefore I shall spare you a direct analysis of his work. May I only refer very briefly to Tasso's peculiar way of representing a dream with the consciousness of the dream—the dream of the *Aminta* (*s'ei piace, ei lice*), Tancredi's and Rinaldo's dreams—like the artists who delighted in the conscious "artiness" of their images and compositions, even through conscious distortions, exaggerations, and sophisticated, rhetoricized stylizations.

But we must hurry, for we are mostly interested in taking cognizance of the conspicuous presence of another major manifestation of the Mannerist spirit, this time a collective one, chronologically spanning the whole interval between the *Furioso* and the *Liberata* and even beyond—namely the Petrarchist lyric.[10] The import of a change of perspective in this particular case may be even greater than for Tasso, not only because of the high incidence of literary echoes enjoyed by the Petrarchist phenomenon in all of Europe throughout the sixteenth and seventeenth centuries, but, more directly, because the attempts to relate Petrarchism and even Petrarch himself to Baroque proper have so far raised more problems than they have been able to solve.[11]

This desirable reassessment postulates a comprehensive definition of Mannerism which can satisfy the literary historian. Of course, as we all know, *maniera* meant personal and individual style in Vasari's terminology; but in the emphasis the epoch placed on it it became, through the imitation of a master's *maniera,* "*manierismo,*" stylization, convention extended to a whole movement or school. This seems to apply fairly enough to Petrarchism and Bembism. But more specifically, one basic element of differentiation between Mannerism and Baroque lies in the intellectualism of the former as against a prevalence of passion and emotion in the latter. Thus, for example, even though such a theorist of the second half of the Cinquecento as Francesco Patrizi might speak of *entusiasmo* in his attempt to define the substratum of poetic activity, it behooves us to keep in mind that this enthusiasm is not the meta-rational, intuitive or fantastic inspiration through emotion of the Baroque artist. It is an enthusiasm for the rational labors of the cold intellect, as Patrizi showed in his approving analysis of the first fifty sonnets in the *Rime* of Luca Contile (a poet characterized by a calculated tension toward an artful "perfection"). Again Patrizi showed his characteristic bias in the position he took toward the Ariosto-Tasso polemic. The visibly perturbed, obsessive world of Tasso had little to say to this extreme rationalist, who found satisfaction and mental rest in the broad, clear phenomenology of Ariosto's plots and forms: a timeless and changeless world apparently not subjected to human passions.[12] Paradoxically enough, Patrizi's defence of Ariosto leans on his theoretical critique of the Aristotelian poetic categories, which he strives to demolish from within, starting with the principles of imitation and even of rules in general. In a way characteristic of all Mannerism, his restiveness toward the "rules" as guidelines to be surpassed and violated when the personal inspiration so wills, makes him cherish the supreme freedom of Ariosto, while he has no taste for a Tasso who, although he eventually broke more rules than perhaps anyone else, always did so in spite of himself, with consequent deep personal anguish, for in those rules his mind and his conscience very earnestly *believed.*

More specifically still, Mannerism is a fundamental aestheticism which, short of art for art's sake, seeks refuge into an aristocratic, hermetically sealed, introspective world of refinement, away from a troubled and disappointing external world (the social realities of the Italian wars and the Reformation, which were bringing to ruination the beautiful Renaissance ideals of an Abbey of Thélème erected on a humanity made truly human by education and culture).[13]

This refinement and intellectual play, nourished on artiness and metaphysics, occasionally in the form of wit and conceit, takes advantage to some extent of two heterogeneous yet equally usable traditions still active through the century, namely Ficino's sophisticated Platonism and the overelaborated forms of the late flamboyant Gothic.[14] Almost as conspicuously as in the literary sphere, that Platonism also flows through Botticelli and some of Rafael's work into the spiritually rarefied atmospheres of some mystically oriented paintings of the Mannerists. The Gothic elements, in turn, are eminently at work in the aristocratic appeal to courtly audiences within the Ferrarese chivalric romances; in the visual arts, these elements combine with the French influences out of the school of Fontainebleau to condition some exquisite preciosities from the elongations of Parmigiano to the jeweller's touches of a Cellini even in the pedestal of the Perseus.[15]

Let us now take up some specific examples of Petrarchist poetry. We might begin with such gems of metaphysical complication as Galeazzo di Tarsia's (ca. 1520–1553) address of the inner image of the beloved speaking to the lover:

> Ambi vivi in altrui, morti in voi stessi,
> ella di te e tu di lei sembianza
> rendete, come suol limpido specchio.[16]

We can place this testimony alongside that of Gaspara Stampa (ca. 1523–1554), where she says:

> Signor, io so che'n me non son più viva,
> e veggo omai ch'ancor in voi son morta. . . .
> Strano e fiero miracol veramente,
> ch'altri sia viva, e non sia viva, e pèra,
> e senta tutto e non senta nïente;
> sì che può dirsi la mia forma vera,
> da chi ben mira a sì vario accidente,
> un'imagine d'Eco e di Chimera.[17]

The splendid final *arguzia* closes, in magnificent exploitation of mythological references, a running conceit on the notion of the lover's soul leaving its body in order to go and dwell in the beloved—where it finds a "second" death if the love is not returned.

We come across this "miracle" again and again, as, for one last example, in Angelo di Costanzo (1507–1591):

> . . . Troppo sarei crudele e fiera
> soffrendo che di fame entro il mio regno,
> chi per me è fuor del suo, languisca e pèra.[18]*

The conceit was far from gratuitous. It stemmed directly from the cultural tradition established by Ficino's *Commentary on "The Banquet,"* where after entering the distinction of unrequited love and mutual love, he stated that in the former the lover suffers total death, since the spirit leaves him without being received by the beloved, whereas in the latter the spirit resuscitates as soon as it is received by the beloved and recognizes itself in him or her. The metaphysical thought was indeed turned neatly into a conceit and a witticism by Ficino himself who concluded in rapture: *O felice morte alla quale seguitano due vite!* "Oh happy Death, which is followed by two lives!"[19] It was Castelvetro who theoretically wedded Ficino's idea to Petrarchism by elaborating on that idea more explicitly than ever before in a commentary to Petrarch. He chose for this purpose Petrarch's sonnet *Quando giugne per gli occhi al cor profondo,* to the effect that "the Lover's Soul leaves his body, and thus leaves him dead, in order to take new abode in the Beloved, where it will live henceforth if she will receive it."[20] It was a serious intellectual game, but a game nonetheless. On it was based, to some extent, the basic Petrarcho-Platonic assumption that only a sexually frustrated love could be an inextinguishable and reliable passion and that, concomitantly, the "cruel" beloved fulfills the true interest of both her lover and herself by so maintaining and preserving

---

* "The beloved acknowledges she owes loving care to the lover's heart which, leaving its owner's bosom, has taken abode in her own bosom."

true passion—since satisfying the desire would be morally and psychologically injurious to both. Leone Ebreo had said that much, and all too effectively.[21] Now Baldacci has convincingly argued that the crucial knot in this evolution can be located in Bembo's *Asolani* (1505), and I can find no more telling index of the Manneristic orientations to come than Bembo's sophistication of the doctrinal basis of the poem through a dialectic casuistry of love which already contained the recognizable ingredients of the most conscious metaphysical *concettismo*. Thus Bembo (1470–1547) spoke, for example, both in prose and verse of his heart being threatened by love through the dry fire of passion and the damp tears of grief, which neutralized each other somehow and saved him from sure death: in conclusion, the lover "is kept alive by two deaths, and therefore lives, because he dies twice." Or, which is the same in verse, "Who ever saw such fate: / A man being kept alive through a double death?"[22] Of course there is Petrarch behind all this, but the bard of Arezzo had never turned his conceits into a metaphysical doctrine which could survive outside the verse, as it did in Bembo.

The betrayal, as it were, of Petrarch's authentic modules could also be effected in an opposite manner, by turning his psychological drama into lighter moods of refined entertainment. In sonnet 36, *S'io credesse per morte essere scarco*, Petrarch had complained that he could not even hope for relief from suicide, since he was afraid of Hell. Gaspara Stampa transferred this Christian mood to an exquisite courtly conceit: Her suffering is unbearable, yet she will endure it for she does not trust that death can free her. She knows death cannot because she has already "died" (metaphorically) several times, and every time her desire has grown stronger. The treatment of the pun is delightfully sophisticated, but the intellectual game could not be more remote from Petrarch's earnest reflexiveness. The conceit has been turned into a witticism. Furthermore, the distinction between things and words, reality and imagination is dissolved through the confusion of literal and metaphorical.

> S'io credesse por fine al mio martire,
> certo vorrei morire;
> perché una morte sola
> non occide, consola.
> Ma temo, lassa me, che dopo morte
> l'amoroso martir prema più forte;
> e questo posso dirlo, perché io
> moro più volte, e pur cresce il desio.
> Dunque per men tormento
> di vivere e penar, lassa, consento.[23]

Let us now turn our attention to a sonnet by Giovanni Della Casa (1503–1556) which has long been praised, and still is, as one of the earliest in a group which supposedly anticipates the Baroque in a metaphysical vein:

> Le chiome d'or, ch'Amor solea mostrarmi
> per maraviglia fiammeggiar sovente
> d'intorno al foco mio puro, cocente
> (e ben avrà vigor cenere farmi),
>   son tronche, ahi lasso: o fera mano e armi
> crude e o levi mie catene e lente!
> Deh come il signor mio soffre e consente
> del suo lacciuol più forte altri il disarmi?
>   Qual chiuso in orto suol purpureo fiore,
> cui l'aura dolce, e 'l sol tepido, e 'l rio
> corrente nutre, aprir tra l'erba fresca;
>   tale, e più vago ancora, il crin vid'io,
> che solo esser devea laccio al mio core.
> Non già ch'io, rotto lui, del carcer esca.[24]

We are indeed reminded of the Baroque stress on strong visual effects by the metaphorical conceits of the "golden locks which flame up" around the lady's face, itself a "burning fire" to the poet, and again by the hair, "the only effective chain to the poet's heart," striking his eyes like a red flower which stands out among the blades of grass in an enclosed garden, and once again, by the felicitous witticism of the last line, designed to catch us by surprise. Also like the Baroque is the emphatic reliance on a rich, sonorous rhythm, made majestic by the vast fluctuations and sweeping movements underlined by Casa's celebrated use of enjambment. Gravina had already singled out these peculiarities of rhythm[25] and had identified these elements of Casa's "new style" as Horatian in nature.

Yet it will not get us very far to explain the interest and value of all these new modes as an anticipation of Baroque. The Baroque poets had them because, in part, they drew inspiration from Casa and many other Mannerists, but in a different context and for different ends. Casa was expressing a need that finds its *raison d'être* in his own time, not in a later one. In breaking out of the subdued, now conventionalized modalities of Petrarch, Casa was like those painters and architects whose Mannerism consisted of a rebellion against the excessive reliance on the rules, or "examples," of the previous masters, so that they started to use their forms without regard to their logical traditional functions. Casa's strong visual metaphors strike the imagination beyond the logical justification of their conventional meaning just as do the sublimely, violently unfunctional "indoor" windows and hanging piers of Michelangelo's vestibule to the Laurentian Library, or the drooping sections of the overhang in Giulio Romano's Palazzo del Té.

Now I seem to hear the objection that it is contradictory, or at least inconsistent to find Mannerism in both the Petrarchism of Bembo's school and the "anti-Petrarchism" of Casa, or, to put it differently, to find it in both the systematic imitation of a model (in a conventionalized "manner") and the implicit revolt against it.[26] Yet everybody knows that there are not one but several Mannerisms, like Lovejoy's Romanticisms and perhaps more plausibly so. They all have in common the withdrawal from a world of active, naive participation in the exhilarating experience of man's noble show of his virtues and forces—a withdrawal brought about by the crash of the humanistic illusions in the horrors and doubts of wars and religious schism. The "manner" of Bembo was to cling to literature away from life, which is what we call literary academy (and later criticism held Bembo responsible above all others for the "academic" character of much of Italian literature); that

of Casa consisted of rejecting the established literature of the
models in order to find new ways, without, however, resorting
to a new direct look on reality and life but taking refuge in a
new literariness of metaphysical, abstract forms, which tran-
scend the poverty of reality and supply a higher sense for our
existence. The portraits of the real would come out distorted,
like the exasperated metaphors of locks burning on a burning
face, like the disturbingly and madly revolutionary self-portrait of Parmigianino in front of a convex mirror.

The aesthetic closeness of the lyric to the figurative arts
is reflected in the growing preoccupation with the visual aspect
of representation. A heightened sense of pictorial values marks
the Cinquecento lyric and will of course become obsessive in
the synaesthetic orientation of the Baroque. The evolution
from Petrarch to his imitators is in this sense exemplary.
Petrarch's use of visual elements was always rigorously sub-
ordinated to his concentration on the inner experience, the
phenomena of an exquisitely contemplative psyche; corre-
spondingly, the subdued quality of his expression denied access
to overly conspicuous exteriorities. His followers were less
true to this intimate, introspective message, and more overtly
sensual in their representation. They mused a lot, but they
painted more. An example shall suffice. Take the famous
theme of love's stubborn lingering at the poet's side in spite
of the poet's desperate looking for solitude:

> Ma pur sì aspre vie né sì selvagge
> cercar non so, ch'Amor non venga sempre
> ragionando con meco, ed io con lui.[27]

Casa:

> Cangiai con gran mio duol contrada e parte, . . .
> ma già perch' io mi parta, erma e lontana
> riva cercando, Amor da me non parte.[28]

But hear now Galeazzo di Tarsia:

> Ma perch'io vada o dove folto e spesso
> stuolo si prema, o dove uom non s'annide,
> il mio fiero tiranno ognor m'è appresso:

[133]

e s'io cavalco, ei su gli arcion si asside;
se l'onda solco, in su del legno istesso
mel veggio a fianco, e che di me si ride.[29]

The powerfully intimate detail of Petrarch's *ragionare* is replaced by Casa's dramatic finality, but Tarsia places everything upon a vivid stage—without loss of effectiveness.

It has been pointed out that during Bembo's generation the commentators on Petrarch saw in him especially the high master of stylistic moderation, discipline, and direct clarity, whereas their successors started to stress his rhetorical boldness in hyperboles, puns, and metaphors. It is an important distinction, which underlines the gradual turning away from a reading in a classicistic key toward a growing expressivism wary of formal balance—this individualistic expressivism being typical of mature Mannerism even in painting.[30] Incidentally, this vast production of Petrarchan commentaries is, by its very extension and nature, indicative of another phenomenon recently acknowledged as typical of Mannerism, to wit the reflexive, learned consciousness of the purely formal and aesthetic values in one's own and others' poetry. In the Cinquecento both literati and artists constantly analyze, explain, and justify themselves or their models.

As part of the movement toward an academic use of literature, the Petrarchist tradition (and Casa more than Bembo) raised the level of Petrarch's discourse from a "discoursive and plain one" to the "sustained and grave," from *discorrente e piano* to *ritenuto e grave* as Scipione Ammirato pointed out while dealing with the emblems.[31] Now, emblematic literature, which in the Cinquecento and later profusely exploited Petrarch by lifting all sorts of mottos and sayings from his verses, was, once again in a way typical of the Manneristic playing with "literariness," another testimony of the "dissociation of Petrarch's forms from their spiritual substance" (somewhat like the classical moldings used without regard to their logical function and context, simply for their decorative and expressive value).[32] This literature of emblems (with Paolo Giovio, Scipione Ammirato, Scipione Bargagli, Girolamo Ruscelli, Andrea Alciato, down to Giovanni Cisano—1610) also drew upon the other major lyrical work by Petrarch, the *Trionfi*, which however appealed more directly to the vast allegorical constructions known as "theaters" (Marzot mentions in this respect Casoni's *Della magia d'Amore*, Camillo's *La Idea del Teatro*, and A. F. Doni's *Pitture*).[33] To these machinations in print the *Trionfi* lent itself well, since it was, as De Sanctis put it, "a large baroque conceit, or rather a big witticism (*freddura*)*."* It lent itself but it was not the same thing, for clearly new is the emphasis on the game of *ingegno* or wit now exercised on a heightened sense of physical images in their association with religious and moral values. The peculiarly evanescent quality of Petrarch's objective allusions no longer satisfied the ebullient imaginations and the new sensuality.

The taste for the bizarre, the eccentric, and even the monstrous and plainly ugly has, along with other factors, prompted some critics to indulge in comparing Mannerism not only with Baroque but even Romanticism and Decadentism (so do Hocke and Hauser). This concerns "content." On the side of "form" we find, somewhat similarly, a taste for hermeticism or obscurity, which, at least in the form of emblematic literature, could even draw upon the apparently implausible ancestry of Petrarch's verses in spite of their conspicuous virtues of clarity and neatness. Time does not allow me to indulge in more than a couple of examples. One *impresa* shows a heap of coal burning through cracks in the earth covering it, and the motto reads *Tectus magis:* obvious reference to Petrarch's *chiusa fiamma è più ardente* (ca. 207). To be understood the legend *Di fuor si legge* accompanying a figure of the Aetna spewing flames is obviously to be integrated with the remainder of Petrarch's line from sonnet 35, to wit *com'io dentro avvampi* ("one can read on my face how I burn inside").

If we look more closely to the linguistic features affecting lyrical style, we cannot refrain from considering the extreme liberties with word order, the systematic hyperbata which characterized the language of Italian poetry more than any other in

Europe, and which contributed, together with the peculiarities of vocabulary, both to the separation between poetic and prosaic language and to the academic character of the Italian literary tradition—two phenomena in which Italy, once again, exceeded all other countries in Europe, and not for her greater glory. Now will it be improper to identify (or stigmatize, if you will) this notorious insistence on hard grammatical disjointments as a contribution of Cinquecento Mannerism? Here again it is not so much the label that matters, although a label can be useful in order to give collective identity to an historical constant whose precise function differed both from its precedents and its consequents. Hyperbata were popular in ancient languages for reasons of their own nature; they were popular again in some productions of the Middle Ages—Latin and vernacular as well—in which a drastic effort was being made to distinguish an elect elocution from the plainness of more current language, in the wake of admired ancient models. Even then it was felt as an artifice, to be censured in the more infelicitous occurrences as "synchisis" (a pejorative term already used by late Roman grammarians). Transpositions and inversions became particularly frequent in the Italian vernacular in the course of the Quattrocento, and the reason then was the effort, in the climate of Humanism, to bring the vernacular up to the "cultured" standards of classical Latin. They clearly were a case of violence being done to the language, and the more mature prose of a later time wisely and naturally proceeded to drop them by and large. This the special language of verse did not do, just as (once again in the wake of Bembo) the grandiloquent prose of Boccaccio's imitators rescued that pattern from the merciful death the natural evolution of the language tended to reserve for it. This therefore meant, all in all, clinging to something that had lost its dialectical historical function, to wit a fashion, a "manner." We sense the sophisticated grimace of an elegant dandy when we encounter such speakers in the Cinquecento, whereas we appreciated the effort of rising to admired, though relatively alien, standards in the serious exercises of, say, a Leon Battista Alberti. I shall give only a couple of examples, from one of the more respectable Cinquecentisti, Galeazzo di Tarsia, and both will be eloquent cases of drastic synchisis: *Ove più ricovrare, Amor, poss' io/ da' tuoi spesso che ordir lacci mi suoli?* ("Where ever can I recover, O Love, from those fetters of yours which you are so often wont to weave for me?" But the Italian order gives: "Where ever recover, O Love, can I from your that often to weave fetters for me you are wont?") ; . . . *Quando il Franco pel varco, a' nostri danni, / che il gran Moro additò, strada si aperse (= pel varco che il gran Moro additò si aperse la strada a' nostri danni)*.[34] The practice, as is well known, had far-reaching consequences, and was only defeated in the course of the Romantic revolt. But the habit was carried on until that late date because it was strengthened by the new Classicism of the seventeenth and eighteenth centuries. Especially in this phase the phenomenon crossed all natural boundaries: Milton is the most shining example of it, and his was as much a case of violence to the spirit of his language as anyone's in Italy. Let me point out, in ending this argument, that the difference between neoclassic hyperbaton and Manneristic hyperbaton lies precisely in the fact that the former is also, in part, a passive and stale response to an established fashion, but, at least at its best, "revitalized" and justified by a serious classicistic commitment, as precisely in Milton and, for Italy, Parini. To put it in a nutshell, at the risk of oversimplifying, I am inclined to say that Milton's and Parini's hyperbata are inspired by a will toward sustained, noble gravity, those of Tarsia by a desire for the bizarre. Yet there was also another serious side to this practice. Shearman recalls an interesting critical point in Malespini's (Lorenzo Giacomini) 1595 funeral oration for Tasso. The new "Tacitian" taste called for a certain amount of obscurity, and word order could fittingly contribute to this planned obscurity, i.e., when words were "artificially interwoven more than is normal," when they presented frequent "convolutions" and "displacements." In this Tasso had excelled, for, "understanding that perfect clarity is nothing but superabundant ease towards too sudden understanding without giving the listener the opportunity to experience something for himself, [he] . . . sought for his poem . . . not the greatest clarity."[35]

The evolution of Petrarchism is not simply a story of imitation of a model. It is rather the story of this model's impact on successive generations, each one with its own needs. That of Bembo was a movement toward sobriety and moderation (methodically selecting Petrarch's "milder" metaphors) in reaction against the *précieux* "*grande rhétorique*" of Gareth, Tebaldeo, and above all Serafino (heavily playing on striking metaphors and conceits, the "fire" and "ice" antitheses and so forth), whose lesson was, in turn, to be resumed by the Southern Petrarchism, when such Neapolitan lyricists as Isabella di Morra, Galeazzo di Tarsia, Luigi Tansillo, and Angelo di Costanzo aligned themselves with the currents that were dissolving Bembism from within.[36] Suffice, for an example, Tansillo's symptomatic verse *pur ch'in voi doppi il bel, doppi in me il male:* a heavy pun, strengthened by the phonetic pattern of alliterative quality, overdoes the musical suggestions available in Petrarch, and surfaces as a central knot in a supreme exercise of passionate wit (*se mille volte il giorno*).[37]

Thus the second half of the century witnesses a lyric which, rather than anti-Petrarchist, is anti-Bembist, for it seeks more dramatic and more personal experiences. This matches that new individualism which was already announced in the heroic inspiration of Vasari's treatment of the evolution of art as a succession of personal conquests.[38] The intellectual concentration of the first Mannerist wave gives way to a new concern with personal sentimental experiences. The themes of detachment from the world, the vanity of our passions, and the final, frightful solution of it all by death draws formal inspiration from Petrarch's melancholy muse, but goes beyond it in a new, personally, dramatically felt urgency. The realization of the unreality of the real, of the hollowness of our physical environment, of the emptiness of our mundane strivings, which grows from Casa through Celio Magno, matches the Pyrrhonism of the visual artists and of such foreign masters as Montaigne.[39]

A full investigation of our subject should enter a detailed analysis of the use of sundry rhetorical devices taken over from Petrarch in the course of the sixteenth and seventeenth centuries. It would be a long discourse indeed. We only have time to linger on one example, and be content with that for its exemplary character. Antithesis as used by Petrarch (*crudel-pietosa, dolce-amara, ardo da lunge e agghiaccio da presso . . .*) was bound to strike his readers as a revelation, to the extent that it was a fitting outer sign of that contradictory nature of the inner psyche—the "subconscious" ignoring the law of non-contradiction—which Petrarch in the *Secretum* and the *Canzoniere* had turned into a personal, "modern" way of life. Of course antithesis *per se* belongs to no style in particular, yet it makes little difference that the device was, as such, recognized and recommended by a host of rhetoricians starting perhaps with Aristotle, and that it was a standard means of achieving balance in the more or less Isocratean prose of the Gorgian figures. In expressing through antithesis the basic, permanent conflict in his own psyche, Petrarch turned that device into a stylistic correlative to a dialectical tension, an expressive *chiaroscuro*, a psychological *sfumato*. The antithesis was not signally exploited by the schools of Bembo and Casa. But it came boldly to the fore of public favor at the end of the century, and then it became something essentially different from Petrarch's vehicle for psychological insights: it became the core element on which to build daring, showy metaphors and conceits, in a nonchalant display of restive wit. Tasso quoted examples from Petrarch to justify his *calda neve* ("warm snow," the lady's neck), and, typically, Guido Casoni (*Della Magia d'Amore,* 1596) defined the nature of love in terms destined to reappear in Marino's *Adone,* namely "blind Lynx" and "blind-folded Argus."[40]

What the Petrarchists did with that essential feature of Petrarchism in whatever form, namely its dedication to antithetic treatment, is quite interesting: they took away some of its psychological earnestness, and expanded its tendency to be treated through an inherent conceit, as with Weckherlin, for whom Petrarch's precedent operated as a model of systematic and integrated development of the antithesis.[41] In other words, what made Petrarch's antitheses potentially Baroque was their being bent to serve the purpose of a conceit which is extended to run through the entire composition, thus contributing to its total organization on a compositional and stylistic level. But the peculiarly Manneristic way of handling this linguistic-rhetorical situation is one that brings to the fore of our awareness not the truly integrated, organic nature of the conceit as center of the poem: its elements are scattered through the corners of the poem, in a punctual, atomized play on detail. The conceit is continuous and omnipresent, but our attention is distracted from the whole and attracted to the particulars. Nor is this all. Take this typical movement from one of Ariosto's lyrics:[42]

> Come creder debbo io che tu in ciel oda,
> Signor benigno, i miei non caldi prieghi,
> se, gridando la lingua che mi sleghi,
> tu vedi quanto il cor nel laccio goda?*

Almost completely devoid of religious feeling, this use of the traditional Petrarchan theme of the "conversion to God" betrays, in the typically "median" style of this sublimely "bourgeois" poet, the intellectual delight of an ambiguous situation. The Petrarchan struggle (antithetically expressed) between two conflicting and equally insuperable psychological drives is now enjoyed for the subtlety of the presentation, nothing more than an aesthetic thrill.

It is curiously rewarding to find that the correspondence between the literary use of structural patterns and Mannerist art, which has only recently begun to be stressed again, was already recognized by the contemporaries. Both literati and artists drew attention to the systematic use of *contrapposti* (= antitheses and formal contrasts of parts—the figure was also attributed to Petrarch), and to their further evolution in

---

* "How can I presume that You will heed in Heaven, O Lord, my prayers, which are far from fervent, if, while my tongue cries out for freedom, You can see how much my heart rejoices in its fetters?"

what came to be called the *serpentinato,* or "twisted pattern" of composition.[43] Shearman has recalled that in 1540 Vasari sent to Pietro Aretino a drawing of *The Israelites collecting the Manna* in order to "demonstrate the finer points of art." In reply, and accepting this aesthetically self-conscious, formalistic context of the gift, Aretino singled out for comment "the figure bending down . . . which shows at once the back and the front so that it is, by virtue of its easy forcefulness and by grace of its forced ease, a magnet to the eye" (*in virtù de la forza facile e con grazia de la sforzata facilitade*). The conceit applies well to a *figura serpentinata*—a convoluted posture which was specifically condemned in Alberti's *Della Pittura* (1435), namely figures showing both back and front. The Mannerists did prize this posture, as in Paolo Pino's *Dialogo della Pittura* (1548): "The attitudes of figures should be varied and graceful, and in all your works you should introduce at least one figure that is all distorted, ambiguous and difficult, so that you shall thereby be noticed as outstanding by those who understand the finer points of art." It is important to distinguish this taste for the pyramidally contorted from the well known Baroque spiral composition. For Mannerism does not show true movement in dynamic effort, but rather a static posture of elegant complication.

Similarly, the literary theorists recognized both the new emphasis on pure form and the specific taste for antithetic artifices. Thus Tasso expounded a Manneristic deformation of classical theory when he admonished that "the form must not be ordered in function of the subject-matter, nor be dependent on it; rather, it must be the other way around."[44] In turn Guarini underlined the artificiality of his own verse in his commentary to the definitive edition (1602) of the *Pastor Fido* (first performed at Mantua in 1598, but composed in 1586): he pointed out one of the examples of how his verse tended to be most stylized in moments of supposed emotional tension, and praised the following "joining of *contrapposti*" as "a very graceful poetic figure": "E sento nel partire/un vivace morire/ che dà *vita* al dolore/per far che *mora im-*

mortalmente il core." (Act iii: Mirtillo, repulsed by Amarilli.) If it is true that Rococò rediscovered some Manneristic stratagems, one is unquestionably reminded here of Metastasio's melodramatic soliloquies and asides.

The antithetic view of the world and of reality could lie at the foundation of a genuine, dramatic ethical and metaphysical intuition when the Baroque thinkers took hold of it and bent it to their own purposes. In a passage used by Hocke to exemplify the Manneristic theme of the labyrinth, Gracián described a hero who arrives in the labyrinth of a great city and is warned: "The whole universe is made up of contradictions, and its harmony is made up of disharmonies. . . . All worldly things must be turned upside down if you want to see them under their true light."[45] But even this development which I choose to assign to Baroque rather than to Mannerism has its spiritual roots, or at least formal precedents in such surprising, intentional "distortions" as Parmigiano's self-portrait in front of a convex mirror. And we are reminded of Comenius' glasses that deform the truth, Gracián's magic mirror that turns into chimaeras all that had looked natural—the mirror of disillusionment for it unveils the "labyrinth of intrigues, falsehoods, and chimaeras" which is the world and its deceptive natural realities. All this, in turn, has medieval, "Gothic" precedents, as in the Christian theologico-metaphysical paradox of turning upside down to straighten out what has been made topsyturvy by man's sin.[46]

Giraldi Cintio (himself far from untinted by Manneristic twists) was weary of the excesses of *contrapposti* in the madrigals (the most Manneristic form of polyphony): "These young men lament so much about love. . . . Some are alive with death, others die with life; this one burns in ice, that one is frozen in fire; this one cries out while keeping silence, that one is silent while crying out, and all those things that are impossible in nature appear to be possible for them." (*Discorso sopra il romanzo,* 1549–1554.) Giraldi was against the excesses of Bembism but these censures implied all of Petrarchism. Yet he was not condemning emotion, but the artificial representation of a literary, "arty" emotionalism.

This introduces the question of the author's intention and audience's reactions: we can answer it at the same time that we solve a problem which concerns a different subject matter. Horace's *Ars poetica* had raised serious objections to fantasies and monsters. Francesco Luisino's 1554 edition of the *Ars* has a gloss wherein the poet is said to be free to invent whatever he pleases, for his invention is nothing but fiction, and as such it does not affect us: "In just the same way we are not moved by pictures, whether they represent frightening things or pleasant, since it is clear to us that they are fictitious."[47] This, I would submit, fits in with the objective aloofness and skeptical detachment with which Ariosto, and even Boiardo, tend to dominate their fictional world. On his part Shearman further points out that "It makes much better sense of Giulio's monstrosities—the collapsing Hall of the Giants, or the slipping keystones of the Palazzo del Té—to suppose that the sixteenth-century beholder did not believe them for a moment, that he remained unmoved except for a *frisson* of delight in a peculiar kind of beauty."

Shearman tends to see in a similar light the puzzling case of the Sacred Grove of Bomarzo near Viterbo. Vicino Orsini, its owner and inspirer (part author), placed inscriptions on his monsters to label them as such for the benefit of the visitor. And conclusively we read at the far end of the walk, near the preposterous "tilted house," as a key to the whole show, the emblem: *Sol per sfogar il core:* "Solely for the recreation of the spirit."[48]

Bernardo Tasso was Orsini's friend. Another man of letters, Ben Jonson, is adduced by Shearman as a fitting literary counterpoint to his analysis of these curious phenomena. Jonson's *Masque of Queens* (1609) contains an "ougly Hell" complete with witches as an *hors d'oeuvre*, justified by the author as "a spectacle of strangeness, producing multiplicitie of gesture," etc. The classic goals of eloquence were *docere, movere,* and *delectare*—to teach, to move, and to please. The classicists of old and of the High Renaissance as well seemed to be particularly preoccupied with teaching, at least insofar as they were trying to justify their art to themselves. The Baroque will carry the emotional impact beyond the bounds previously acceptable. But in Mannerism delight tends to take the upper hand and become a sufficient end in itself.[49] This could even go to the extreme of a type of "beautiful" language, especially in verse, which carries a minimum of meaning because it starts from the intention of achieving beautiful style, not "expression." Giraldi censured it, and Bembo was sometime accused of it. But its partisans could allege the authority of Demetrius, then a popular rhetorician, to sanction it. One could also, along such lines, sin against the principle of decorum or correspondence of style to meaning, since one would care for a certain style regardless of subject matter. The norms imposed by the Counter-Reformation to Catholic artists attempted to correct these deviations by insisting on appropriateness of form. Accordingly we have all sorts of criticisms leveled against some Manneristic manifestations in all arts, like the criticism of Masses musically so treated that all parts sounded alike, instead of closely reflecting the changing themes.[50]

The Mannerists, then, were essentially formalists who more often than not displayed an inclination toward the ornate style. This becomes particularly interesting in the light of the strong tendency toward the plain style in some peculiar forms (like the curt or Tacitian, the sententious or Senecan, or even the loose or cut style), which manifested itself polemically in the course of the Baroque age. Speroni, for one, criticized Virgil for not being "as florid and ornamented as he should be; he is therefore more of a historian than a poet. He was studious of brevity, which the poet should avoid. Brevity is incompatible with ornamentation, which is all superabundance." Seeking, then, the virtues of diffusiveness or abundance (*copia* and *amplificatio*), Speroni admired the floridity of Homer, who "certainly gives delight by pleasingly ornamenting and amplifying his works." We have thus a typically Manneristic justification of Aristotelian unity, a paradox of "tortuous classicism": "Since poetry consists in superfluous and redundant ornament, if the poet treats multiple actions poetically, the poem, if it is to be perfect, will grow to infinity."[51] Indeed, Ariosto did threaten, at times, to move toward that kind of "infinity," and for Boiardo we almost feel that, had not death stopped him in mid-course, he could have gone on forever. In a different context Tasso followed Speroni very closely in his own *Discorsi*, and he thought that the *meraviglie* in his *Jerusalem Delivered* were even richer than Homer's.

Yet the historians of Mannerism have not yet tackled the problem of the transition from this ornateness to the plain style of some of the Baroque. For not all Mannerism is ornate (nor, by any means, is all Baroque plain). More crucially, there is a zone in between, in which incipient plainness is still part of Mannerism rather than Baroque. To recall some of the facts, the last generation of the century came under the influence of Justus Lipsius, restorer of Stoicism and European leader of anti-Ciceronianism. His curt, abrupt, asymmetric Latin, fraught with points and conceits, impressed such disparate authors as Montaigne and Sponde, La Ceppède and d'Aubigné. Sponde's original modes have been related to those of the English metaphysicals, who, like Donne, sought a pregnant, sententious brevity, and, by uniting passion and thought, tended toward abstraction (while Baroque tended rather to the concrete).[52]

Now the most salient feature in Donne, Praz insists, is not wit or conceit, but the nervous dialectic of his passionate mind, which finds parallels in Maurice Scève's poetry according to Odette de Mourgues,[53] but ultimately goes back to Petrarch himself, whose sonnet *Quando giunge per gli occhi al cor profondo* describes, for example, the ecstasy of the lovers in terms like Donne's *Extasie*. Praz concludes that if Scève's *Délie* (1544, at the time of the school of Fontainebleau) can be called Manneristic, so must be Donne's amatory verse.

Without a specific attempt to connect them with Mannerism, the correlative and *plurimembre* patterns involved in the peculiar compositive structure of much of Petrarchist poetry have been masterfully studied by Dámaso Alonso.[54] I have referred, above, to the new importance these and other patterns acquired when they became treated systematically as the central principle of organization of the poem. I should now like to recall a few of Alonso's most typical examples and add some from the non-Italian areas for comparison. As extreme cases of Petrarchan imitation Alonso singled out especially Domenico Venier ("M'arde, impiaga, ritien, squarcia, urta e preme/ foco, stral, nodo, artiglio, impeto e peso"—a case of *examembre* correlation on love's damages)[55] and his disciple Luigi Groto ("Co' bei, vivi, aurei, ciglio, occhi, capelli,/ ond'arco, fiamma, rete, ha, trahe, torciglia/ la mia dea . . ."),[56] all leading to Marino (Canto viii, octs. 33–34, and Sonnet to Lilla ("Ma tu sola cagion de' miei cordogli,/ Lilla, la piaga, il foco, il nodo mio,/ ché non sani, non tempri e non disciogli?"—this being the final tercet which recapitulates the first quatrain, containing what stings: *spine, punte, aghi;* the second, containing what consumes: *raggi, facelle;* and the first tercet, containing what shackles: *reti, lacciuoli, ami*). The artificial, Manneristic complication of Petrarch's heritage could not be clearer.

Jean de Sponde (1557–1595) was the chief late Mannerist at a time when the anti-Classicism of Mannerism was being challenged by Malherbe. A quatrain from his *Sonnets de la mort* shows an obsessive use of parallelisms through polysyndetic iteration, with a powerful effect even though the means adopted are a bit too mechanical *(tout, et, dont)* :

> Tout s'enfle contre moi, tout m'assaut, tout me tente,
> Et le monde, et la chair, et l'ange révolté,
> Dont l'onde, dont l'effort, dont le charme inventé
> Et m'abime, Seigneur, et m'ébranle, et m'enchante.

Shakespeare is still the Mannerist who espouses Euphuist and Petrarchist *contrapposti* with a pun-like effect:

> . . . O brawling love! O loving hate!
> O anything of nothing first create!
> O heavy lightness! Serious vanity!
> Mis-shapen chaos of well-seeming forms!
> Feather of lead, bright smoke, cold fire, sick health!

Still-waking sleep, that is not what it is!
This love feel I, that feel no love in this.
(Romeo & Juliet, Act I, Sc. 1)

An interesting case is presented by Lope de Vega's sonnet "De Absalon."

Svspenso esta Absalon entre las ramas,
Que entretexen sus hojas, y cabellos.
Que los que tienen la soberuia en ellos
Iamas espiran en bordadas camas.
Cubre de nieue las hermosas llamas,
Al eclipsar de aquellos ojos bellos.
Que assi quebrantan los altiuos cuellos
Las ambiciones de mayores famas.
Que es de la tierra que vsurpar quisiste,
Pues a penas la tocas de liuiano,
Bello Absalon, famoso exemplo al suelo?
Esperança, ambicion, cabellos diste
Al viento, al cielo, a la ocasion tan vano,
Que te quedaste entre la tierra y cielo.[57]

Gracián[58] found the sonnet a "grave y conceptuoso" example of "la agudeza por ponderación misteriosa." He first gave a general definition of the technique:

Mucho promete el nombre, pero no corresponde la realidad de su perfección; quien dice misterio, dice preñez, verdad escondida y recondita, y toda noticia que cuesta, es más estimada y gustosa. Consiste el artificio desta especie de agudeza en levantar misterio entre la connexión de los extremos, o términos correlatos del sujeto, repito, causas, efectos, adjuntos, circunstancias, contingencias; y después . . . dase una razón sutil . . . La razón que se da al reparo ha de ser ingeniosa, que en ella consiste la principal formalidad desta agudeza; las más agradables son las que se dan por conformidad o correspondencia entre los dos terminos o extremos de la ponderación en que se funda el misterio. . . .

He then reproduced the sonnet and briefly considered its mystery:

Nótese la muchedumbre de correspondencias: entre el quedar en el aire y su vanidad; mejor, entre su ambición de

ocupar la tierra y quedarse al aire; más recóndita,
entre la ocasión calva y sus cabellos, que le fueron lazo
para tan desdichada muerte.

It is an eloquent explanation which illustrates the theoretical principles exposed above.[59]

Generally speaking, repetitive patterns were far from a novelty. Besides all the ancient precedents, they were popular among the *troubadours,* and even Dante showed that he appreciated them in his own unique way. But while, for instance with Dante, they would acquire a mystic value that justified them beyond "literature" (even with acrostics, parallelisms, iterations), in Petrarch they did become obsessively dominant solely for the aesthetic pleasure they could provide.

It must be stressed that this methodic use of structural patterns differs from overall composition—indeed the lack of the latter is as characteristic of Mannerism as is the heavy reliance on the former, these two phenomena being then attendant upon each other. For Mannerism curiously combines a looseness of the whole and a high degree of organization of the parts. This phenomenon, well known to art historians, has a precedent, as it were, *avant la lettre* in Petrarch's consciousness of the way his overelaborate poems were tied together in the *Canzoniere* (*Rerum vulgarium fragmenta* being his title for it, and *Voi ch'ascoltate in rime sparse il suono* its first line). The examples we have just seen were mostly sonnets. The incapacity to "compose" in a global unitary way, or, better, a taste for what we might be tempted to call a cinematic sort of *montage* as opposed to a criterion of finality and necessity in the flowing together of the parts, is best shown by such disparate yet kindred masterpieces (mostly prose, but not exclusively) as *Gargantua and Pantagruel,* the *Don Quixote* (First Part), Montaigne's *Essays,* and Shakespeare's *Antony and Cleopatra.* Cervantes' novel has often been characterized as the most carelessly written of all literary masterpieces (at least in the First Part).[60] We might choose to look upon this type of "looseness" as its title to first place among the masterpieces of Mannerism.

In conclusion I should like to point out one substantive argument in support of any use of labels and categories which need to be defended against the damaging charge of *ex-post-facto*, contemporary arbitrariness—nowadays a fashionable way of excluding any broad historiographic concept from the right of citizenship in the republic of letters. The argument is that not only is the term Mannerism justified by a long historical tradition which goes back even to the contemporaries, but the application of it to literature also can boast the same historical precedents. Indeed, to mention only one, particularly fitting example, Pier Jacopo Martello in his 1710 *Comentario* used *manierista* alongside *petrarchista* and *marinista*, in an interesting parallel between pictorial effects and literary phenomena.[61] Indeed, it is precisely because of greater adherence of art history to contemporaneous theoretical awareness that it may pay to heed the suggestions of art history over an even wider arch of literary history than we have contemplated here, namely from Mannerism all the way through Rococò and Neoclassicism.[62]

NOTES

1. De Sanctis, *Storia della Letteratura Italiana* (2 vols., Bari, 1965⁹), esp. chs. 13 and 15, and "L'uomo del Guicciardini" (1869) in his *Saggi Critici* (Bari, 1969²), vol. III.

2. The most compact presentation of the problems arising from the application of the criteria of Mannerism from art to literature is the bibliographically very rewarding paper by Ezio Raimondi, "Per la nozione di manierismo letterario (Il problema del manierismo nelle letterature europee)," *Manierismo, Barocco, Rococò: Concetti e Termini* (Rome, Accademia Naz. dei Lincei, 1962), pp. 57-79. Elaborate discussions of this current assimilation are found in many of the broad studies of Mannerism in the arts: most recently John Shearman, *Mannerism* (Penguin Books, 1967); Arnold Hauser, *Mannerism: The Crisis of the Renaissance and the Origin of Modern Art*, 2 vols. (London, 1965) [from 1964 German original]). Also see Wylie Sypher, *Four Stages of Renaissance Style: Transformations in Art and Literature, 1400-1700* (Garden City, New York, 1956); Gustav René Hocke, *Die Welt als Labyrinth* (Hamburg, 1957), also in French trans. as *Labyrinthe de l'art fantastique* (Paris, 1967); Id., *Manierismus in der Literatur: Sprach-Alchimie und eso- terische Kombinationskunst* (Hamburg, 1959), also in It. trans. as *Il Manierismo nella letteratura* (Milan, 1965). Compact Italian surveys of the art-historical polemic about Mannerism can also be found in an article by G. Nicco Fasola in *Scritti di Storia dell'Arte in onore di L. Venturi*, I (Rome, 1956); and, more comprehensively, in the chapter "Sfortune del Manierismo" of Eugenio Battisti, *Rinascimento e Barocco* (Torino, 1960), pp. 216-37. Later on Battisti has offered a different terminological framework for the question of Mannerist art in his *L'Antirinascimento* (Milan, 1962). See, also, Robert E. Wolf, "Renaissance, Mannerism, Baroque: Three Styles, Three Periods," *Les Colloques de Wégimont*, IV (1957); *Le 'Baroque' Musical* (Paris, 1963; Université de Liège, 1964), pp. 35-80; and "La discussione sul Manierismo" in Riccardo Scrivano, *Cultura e Letteratura nel Cinquecento* (Rome, 1966), pp. 231-84, con- taining updated bibliographic information and sensible strictures on the use of the historiographic concept of Mannerism. *Colloquia Germanica: Intern. Zeitschrift für germ. Sprach- und Literaturwiss.*, I (1957) contains discussions of literary Mannerism by R. Montano, B. L. Spahr, A. G. de Capua, D. A. Carozza, and P. Goff. I have been unable to see the recent Klaus-Peter Lange, *Theoriker des literarischen Manierismus: Tesauros und Pellegrinis Lehre von der Acutezza oder von der Macht der Sprache.* Hum. Bibl. I, 4 (Munich, (1968).
   To the preceding titles, all in some way concerned with a parallel treat- ment of literature and the arts, I should also add two recent broad studies which extend themselves to the whole of the European scene, namely: Franz- sepp Würtenberger, *Mannerism, The European Style of the Sixteenth Century*, trans. M. Heron (New York, 1963; German original Vienna, 1962); and Jacques Bousquet, *Mannerism*, trans. S. W. Taylor (New York, 1964).

3. This is not the place to go into the complex question of the para- or meta-historical relationship between either Mannerism or Baroque and modern poetry, such as Symbolism, Decadentism, Expressionism, Hermeticism, and especially Surrealism. But since some of the investigators of literary-artistic Mannerism (and some of the best among them, such as E. R. Curtius, G. Hocke, and A. Hauser) have slanted their analysis of past forms on the assumption of such a relationship with contemporary ones, it will not be amiss to note the problem at least in passing. And we may want to take the

position, just for the record, that we have no more than an interest of curiosity in registering this critical phenomenon to which we must deny any validity beyond that of arousing the audience's interest through provocative but critically hollow associations. Haskell Block has given an exemplary warning on the unsoundness of the rapprochement between metaphysicals and symbolists, and we may temporarily feel satisfied with his contribution. See H. M. Block, "The Alleged Parallel of Metaphysical and Symbolist Poetry," *Comp. Lit. Studies,* IV (1967), 145–59. Block may have overstressed the objection of personal "individuality" in the poets as against their formal similarities from age to age; but more fundamentally, and on a deeper level perhaps, it is the imperative of the proper historical perspectives which forbids us to yield to such associations without regard to time-bound meanings within precise contexts.

4. Cf. the first systematic, though tentative, treatment of the literary Cinquecento from this new angle, Riccardo Scrivano's *Il Manierismo nella letteratura del Cinquecento* (Padua, 1959), and the strictures advanced in the review by Dante Della Terza, "Manierismo nella letteratura del Cinquecento," *Belfagor,* XV (1960), 462–66. But see the immediately successive, and more concretely rewarding, Georg Weise, "Manierismo e letteratura," *Riv. di Letterature Moderne e Comparate,* XIII (1960), 5–52. The more recent volume by Scrivano offers mature and well-informed insights into several aspects of the subject: *Cultura e Letteratura nel Cinquecento,* esp. 231–84.

5. The cut-off point between Mannerism and Baroque should be kept, in my judgment, as close to the end of the Cinquecento as possible (just as the beginning of it in literature appears most convincing when we make it coincide with the generation that flourished after 1520). Of course, Mannerist orientations may continue to be visible in the course of the seventeenth century: the term can then remain useful to introduce further distinctions within a culture generally dominated by Baroque trends. John Donne, e.g., has been successfully assessed as Manneristic in his lyrics and Baroque in his sermons.

6. Raimondi, "Per la nozione di manierismo letterario," p. 74. Cf. Ulrich Leo, *T. Tasso. Studien zur Vorgeschichte des Secentismus* (Bern, 1951). But on the merits of this work see, e.g., my review in *Italica,* XXXI, 2 (1954), 120–25. Also cf. F. Chiappelli, "Tassos Stil im Uebergang von Renaissance zu Barock," *Trivium* (1949), 286–309; and see, now, Ferruccio Ulivi, *Il Manierismo del Tasso e altri studi* (Florence, 1966).

7. Cf. the introduction to my edition of Boiardo's *Orlando Innamorato e Amorum Libri* (Torino, 1963), Vol. I, and my "Chivalric and Idyllic Poetry in the Italian Renaissance," *Italica,* XXXIII, 4 (1956), 252–60.

8. More detailed remarks on the texture of cosmos-chaos in the *Mad Roland* in my *Nature and Love in the Late Middle Ages* (Berkeley-Los Angeles, 1963), pp. 133–34.

9. Battisti, *Rinascimento e Barocco,* pp. 233–34, has hinted at the contrast between two ways of relating Ariosto to his socio-cultural context with possible appeals to art-historical categories, to wit: Arminio Janner, "Il Castiglione e l'Ariosto a sostegno di Enrico Wölfflin," *Concinnitas: Beiträge zum Problem des Klassischen. H. Wölfflin zum 80. Geburtstag, 1944* (Basel, 1944), 117–36; Antonio Piromalli, *La Cultura a Ferrara al tempo di L. Ariosto* (Florence, 1953) and *Motivi e forme della poesia di L. Ariosto* (Messina-Florence, 1954). Janner attempted to tie Castiglione and Ariosto to Raphaël's suave gracefulness and simple grandeur; above all he played on the anti-individualistic exaltation of the courtier as a member of an elite group, absorbed into it through his "honest mediocrity," the common, median line "without ex-

Aldo Scaglione

tremes in any part" (even in the dress), which adopts social uniformity as a supreme rule. Piromalli, on the other hand, has recalled the restiveness and misery hidden behind the princely luxuries of Ariosto's Ferrara. It seems also in order to recall here the cult of refinement encouraged by the Court of Ferrara, which is one sense of *maniera* in the terminology of the time. Ariosto's "alto sembiante e divine maniere," "altiera e umana maniera," B. Tasso's and T. Tasso's "peregrino" and "raro" respond to an exaltation of the strange and elegantly unusual rather than of the natural, simple, and direct. The origin of this trend toward refinement was French, from the late Gothic courtly chivalry thriving in the romances as well as in manners under Charles VIII and Louis XII. Cf., in particular, G. Weise, "La doppia origine del concetto di Manierismo," *Studi Vasariani: Atti del Convegno Intern. per il 4° Cent. della Iª ed. delle Vite del Vasari* (Florence, 1952), pp. 181–85, and the further studies by Marco Treves and Luigi Coletti indicated by Battisti, *Rinascimento e Barocco*, 233–34.

10. On Cinquecento Petrarchism see now, especially, Giulio Marzot, "Il tramite del Petrarchismo dal Rinascimento al Barocco," *Studi Petrarcheschi*, VI (1956), 123–75, and Luigi Baldacci, *Il Petrarchismo italiano nel Cinquecento* (Milan-Naples, 1957). Of course, had we only time and space enough, it would be expedient to relate the Petrarchist lyric of the Cinquecento to the Petrarchist, "pre-baroque" courtly lyric of the late Quattrocento. This subject still deserves close and detailed scrutiny, even though it was recognized for its problematic character as early as 1884 in an essay by D'Ancona, *Studi sulla Letteratura Italiana de' primi secoli,* "Del secentismo nella poesia cortigiana del sec. XV" (Ancona, 1884). See, for a particular aspect of the contrast between Bembo and this tradition, Vincenzo Calmeta, *Prose e lettere edite e inedite,* ed. Cecyl Grayson (Bologna, 1959), Introduction; and, also, Georg Weise, "Elementi tardogotici nella letteratura italiana del Quattrocento," *Rivista di Letterature Moderne e Comparate,* X (1957).

11. Cf., for example, Oscar Büdel, *F. Petrarca und der Literaturbarock: Schriften und Vorträge des Petrarca-Instituts Köln,* XVII (Köln, 1963); and my review in *Romance Philology,* XVIII (1965), 360-62.

12. See Patrizi's defense of Ariosto in the *Parere del Sig. F. Patrici in difesa dell'Ariosto,* printed in T. Tasso, *Apologia in difesa della sua Gerusalemme Liberata* (Ferrara, Cagnacini, 1585), as well as the *Trimerone,* last part of Patrizi's *Deca disputata.* Cf. R. Scrivano, "Un momento della lirica cinquecentesca," *La Rassegna della lett. it.,* 62, Ser. vii, 2 (1958), 202–7 on Patrizi's annotations to Contile; and, on the interrelationship between Patrizi's positions concerning poetry, poetics, rhetoric, logic, and politics, see Scrivano, *Il Manierismo,* pp. 57–66. Also Scrivano, *Cultura e Letteratura,* "L. Contile e F. Patrizi," pp. 185–94.

13. Aestheticism is seen as the main aspect of the movement by J. Shearman, *Mannerism,* who, however, refuses to accept the social conditioning of such psychological and artistic attitudes. With this exception, I lean chiefly on Shearman for the art-historical definition of Mannerist features.

14. The Ficinian component of much of Cinquecento Petrarchism has been best highlighted by Luigi Baldacci: see, for the summary examples I give below, his anthology *Lirici del Cinquecento* (Florence, 1957), pp. x–xiv, and more extensively, his *Il Petrarchismo italiano nel Cinquecento,* esp. pp. 86–114.

15. With reference to the neogothic features common to such Quattrocento artists at Botticelli, Filippino Lippi, Pollaiuolo, and reemerging in such first-generation Mannerists as Pontormo, Georg Weise, "Elementi tardogotici nella letteratura italiana del Quattrocento," pp. 101–30 and 184–99, has interpreted

[152]

Cinquecento Mannerism and the Uses of Petrarch

Boiardo's *Innamorato* and the late Quattrocento Petrarchists as forerunners of Mannerism.

16. Galeazzo di Tarsia, *Rime,* ed. D. Ponchiroli (Paris, Tallone, 1951), Sonnet 25.

17. Baldacci, *Lirici del Cinquecento,* pp. xi–xii and 135.

18. Cf. Baldacci, *Lirici,* p. 664.

19. Ficino, *Sopra lo amore ovvero Convito di Platone,* ed. G. Rensi (Lanciano, 1914), pp. 38–39, cited by Baldacci, *Lirici,* p. 664.

20. Petrarca, *Rime* (Basel, P. de Sebadonis, 1582), p. 179, cited by Baldacci, *Lirici,* pp. x–xi.

21. Cf. Baldacci, *Il Petrarchismo,* pp. 101–2.

22. "da due morti è vivo tenuto e, perciò che egli doppiamente muore, egli si vive";

> Chi vide mai tal sorte:
> tenersi in vita un uom con doppia morte?

Cf. P. Bembo, *Gli Asolani e le Rime,* ed. C. Dionisotti (Torino, 1929), pp. 26–27; and Baldacci, *Lirici,* pp. xii–xiii.

23. Baldacci, *Lirici,* p. 158.

24. Cf. Baldacci, *Lirici,* pp. 444–45 (sonnet 8) for the text; I read *esser* rather than *essere* in l. 13 as the only way to restore the hendecasyllable. Baldacci recalls that Seroni singles out the image of "fire on fire" as Baroque.

25. "maestoso giro delle parole, ondeggiamento di numero": cf. V. Gravina, *Ragion poetica* (Rome, 1708), p. 213, cited by Baldacci, *Lirici,* p. 436.

26. Those who apply the category of Mannerism to the lyric (e.g. Scrivano) tend to restrict it to the "anti-Petrarchists" of the second half of the Cinquecento. Against this prevailing trend G. Weise ("Manierismo e Letteratura," cited, esp. pp. 5–19), even though he insists on the necessity to restrict the use of the term within clear historical limits, does not hesitate to designate as Manneristic the whole Petrarchan tradition of antithetic conceits through the Quattrocento and back to Petrarch himself. On the other hand, Weise excludes Bembo from this Manneristic Petrarchism, even while he admits that his immediate followers and, in general, the Cinquecento lyricists tended to combine Bembo's "classical," "sober" brand of Petrarchism with the conceits as well as cerebral witticisms of the late Quattrocento lyricists. In this sense I am here striking a middle course between these two uses of the term.

27. Petrarch, *Canzoniere,* 35 (Sonnet "Solo e pensoso").

28. See G. Della Casa, *Rime,* ed. D. Ponchiroli (Torino, 1967), Sonnet 14, p. 26.

29. Baldacci, *Lirici,* p. 650.

30. Cf. Marzot, "Il tramite del Petrarchismo dal Rinascimento al Barocco," *Studi Petrarcheschi,* VI (1956), esp. pp. 132–33.

31. Dialogue on *Imprese* in S. Ammirato, *Gli Opuscoli* (Florence, 1640), I, 467.

32. Marzot, "Il tramite del Petrarchismo," esp. p. 140.

33. *Ibid.,* p. 147.

34. Cf. Baldacci, *Lirici,* pp. 645 and 652.

35. Shearman, *Mannerism,* pp. 159–61.

36. For a close study of the still elusive context of the clash between Bembo and the late fifteenth-century "pre-Baroque" milieu see Grayson's essay on Calmeta already mentioned.

37. Text in Baldacci, *Lirici,* p. 602. Also, on some of these poets, cf. L.

Baldacci, "Lirici del Cinquecento," in *Inventario*, V, 5–6 (Oct.–Dec., 1953), 84-98.

38. Scrivano, *Il Manierismo*, aptly underlines this new individualism, but in making it the center of Mannerism, almost to the exclusion of every formal feature of that complex phenomenon, he impoverishes it and reduces it to a movement that cannot be identified but very vaguely.

39. Cf., in particular, A. Tenenti, *Il senso della morte e l'amore della vita nel Rinascimento (Francia e Italia)* (Torino, 1957), for aspects of the theme of death between art and literature.

40. *Lince privo di lume, Argo bendato:* see these quotes in Giulio Marzot, "Il tramite del Petrarchismo dal Rinascimento al Barocco," p. 131.

41. For an example, (i.e., *Die Lieb ist Leben und Tod*) see O. Büdel, *F. Petrarca und der Literaturbarock*, pp. 18f.

42. Cf. Baldacci, *Lirici*, p. 254.

43. See Shearman, *Mannerism, passim*, especially pp. 83, 86, 94–95, 99, 151, 157–58 for this and the following points. I should add that Panofsky's interpretation of the *figura serpentinata* as "revolving view" (*Studies in Iconology*, 1939) has been boldly applied by Sypher to the many-faceted hero (such as Hamlet), who has to be viewed from all sides to be comprehended (*Four Stages*, p. 156).

44. "La forma non deve essere ordinata in grazia della materia, né pendere da quella, anzi tutto il contrario." Tasso, *Discorsi dell'arte poetica* (Ferrara, 1587), 3ᵈ Discourse.

45. Cf. G. R. Hocke, *Labyrinthe de l'art fantastique* (1967), pp. 110–11. See *El Criticón* (1651–52) in Gracián, *Obras completas*, ed. Arturo del Hoyo (Madrid, 1960).

46. Cf. Philip Damon, "Geryon, Cacciaguida, and the Y of Pythagoras," *Dante Studies*, LXXXV (1967), 15–32.

47. Shearman's trans., *Mannerism*, p. 157. See also Shearman's following comment.

48. *Ibid.*, p. 158. I am not too sure that Sherman's "recreation of the spirit" is the most appropriate translation for Vicino's *sfogar il core*, but *sol*, "only," is, for our purpose, the key word, and sufficient to underline the aesthetic aloofness of the artist's limited purposes.

49. For an expert discussion of the three goals with particular reference to Baroque see Guido Morpurgo Tagliabue, "Aristotelismo e Barocco," in *Retorica e Barocco, Atti del III Congr. Intern. di Studi Umanistici, 1954* (Rome, 1955), pp. 119–95.

50. Shearman, *Mannerism*, pp. 167–68.

51. Speroni, *Discorsi sopra Virgilio* (ca. 1562), cited by Shearman, *Mannerism*, p. 151.

52. Cf. Alan Boase's important Introduction to Sponde, *Méditations* (Paris, 1954); Louis L. Martz, *The Poetry of Meditation* (New Haven, Conn., 1962²); and Marcel Raymond, "Le Baroque littéraire français," in *Manierismo, Barocco, Rococò*, pp. 107–26, esp. p. 114. The volume *French Manneristic Poetry between Ronsard and Malherbe* of *L'Esprit Créateur*, VI, 4 (1966), 225-97, moves chiefly from Hauser's suggestions (1964–65) and includes H. A. Hatzfeld's "Mannerism is not Baroque," pp. 225–33, and R. M. Burgess, "Mannerism in Philippe Desportes," pp. 270–81.

53. O. de Mourgues, *Metaphysical, Baroque, and Précieux Poetry* (Oxford, 1953), p. 10. Cf. Mario Praz, "Il Barocco in Inghilterra," in *Manierismo, Barocco, Rococò*, pp. 129–46; see esp. p. 140.

54. See, especially, D. Alonso's substantive essay "La poesia del Petrarca e

Cinquecento Mannerism and the Uses of Petrarch

il Petrarchismo: Mondo estetico della pluralità," *Studi Petrarcheschi*, VII (1961), 73–120; also his *Estudios y Ensayos Gongorinos* (Madrid, 1955); D. Alonso and C. Bousoño, *Seis calas en la expresión literaria española* (Madrid, 1951), pp. 29–111.

55. Domenico Venier, *Rime* (Bergamo, 1751), Sonnet 30. Cf. Alonso, "La poesia del Petrarca," esp. pp. 104–6.

56. Cf. Alonso, *Versos plurimembres y poemas correlativos. Capitulo para la estilistica del Siglo de Oro* (Madrid, 1944), p. 132, and his *Estudios . . . Gongorinos*, p. 245.

57. It is Sonnet CIV in Lope de Vega, *La Hermosura de Angelica, con otras diversas Rimas* (Madrid, 1602).

58. *Agudeza y arte de ingenio*, in Gracián, *Obras completas*, ed. Arturo del Hoyo (Madrid, 1960), pp. 260–61.

59. The correlative form by dissemination/recollection of this sonnet, and its relevance to its contemporaries as shown by Gracián, are examined by E. George Erdman, Jr., "Lope de Vega's 'De Absalon,' a *laberinto* of *concetos esparcidos*," *Studies in Philology*, LXV (1968), 753–67.

60. Cf. W. P. Ker, *Collected Essays* (1925), II, 38, adopted by Hauser, *Mannerism*, I, 324.

61. Cf. Gianfranco Folena, "Le origini e il significato del rinnovamento linguistico nel Settecento italiano," in Th. Elwert, *Problemi di lingua e lett. it. del Settecento: Atti del IV Congresso dell'Ass. Intern. per gli studi di Lingua e Lett. It.* (Wiesbaden, 1965), p. 398. Mario Fubini, *Dal Muratori al Baretti* (Bari, 1954²), p. 317, also stresses Martello's parallel between "Marinismo" and the painters' "Mannerism." See, now, the new edition of the *Comentario* on pp. 113–48 of Martello, *Scritti critici e satirici*, ed. H. S. Noce (Bari, 1963). Martello introduces Raphael as saying that the modern poets ought to combine the virtues of Petrarch with those of Marino, just as the modern painters combine Raphael's own virtues with those of the *manieristi*, "especially those of the time of the Caracci" (p. 141). Marino is characterized as *manieroso e dolce* (p. 139).

Similarly, we know how the Italian *Arcadi* of the first half of the eighteenth century turned against the *secentista* style by opposing to it the classicism of the Cinquecento. Yet some shrewd observers managed at that time to perceive the existence, within the sixteenth century, of anti-classical elements which they felt inclined to relate to the Baroque. Thus Francesco Algarotti in his *Lettere sull' 'Eneide' del Caro* censured Caro's famous translation for its puns, witticisms, conceits, and intemperate ornamentation. More interesting still, in the fifth of those letters, he stopped to analyze the frescoes of Giulio's Palazzo del Té and concluded that they were just as remote from the classicism of Raphael as Caro's *Aeneid* was from that of Virgil. Cf. Ettore Bonora, "Obiezioni allo stile prebarocco: Le Lettere sull' 'Eneide' del Caro di F. Algarotti," in *La Critica Stilistica e il Barocco Letterario: Atti del 2° Congresso Int. di Studi It.* [Ass. Int. per gli Studi di Lingua e Lett. It.] (Florence, 1957), pp. 170–76, esp. 175.

62. Cf., e.g., Walter Moretti, "L. Magalotti e il Rococò europeo," *Problemi di Lingua e Letteratura It. del Settecento*, pp. 252–59; and Walter Binni, "Il Rococò letterario," *Manierismo, Barocco, Rococò*, pp. 217–37. For objections to Binni's too broad notion of Rococò see Helmut Hatzfeld, "The Rococo of Goldoni," *Italica*, XLV (1968), 410–20. Sypher has followed up his *Four Stages* with *Rococo to Cubism in Art and Literature* (New York, 1960).

Appendix

Statement of Objectives

The Southeastern Institute of Medieval and Renaissance Studies was established for the advancement of scholarship and improvement of teaching in the southeastern region. Through the Institute the resources of Duke University and the University of North Carolina—particularly library holdings—were made available to scholars and teachers throughout the region. Participation was invited from students of all areas of medieval and renaissance studies, including (among others) art, aesthetics, history, literature, music, philosophy, and religion.

The Institute consisted of six informal seminars, each one concerned with a topic of special interest to students of the medieval and renaissance periods. Each seminar was led by a Senior Fellow and had an enrollment of not more than six participants, designated Fellows. The typical seminar met twice a week for one to two hours, but schedules were flexible to permit arrangements adapted to the needs of the seminar. Each Fellow participated in one seminar and had ample free time to devote to his own research. In addition to the seminars, the Institute sponsored a public lecture by each of the six Senior Fellows and held a daily coffee hour for those Institute members who wished to attend.

The Institute alternated annually between the campuses of Duke University and The University of North Carolina at Chapel Hill. The fifth session, from July 15 to August 22, 1969, was held on The University of North Carolina campus. Fellows were encouraged to use the libraries and other research facilities of both universities.

Seminars of the Fifth Session, July 15–August 22, 1969

1. CHAUCER

Senior Fellow: Dr. Norman E. Eliason, Kenan Professor of English, The University of North Carolina at Chapel Hill. Visiting Professor, University of Innsbruck (1956), King's College, University of London (1962), Duke (1966–67), Univ. of Iowa (summer, 1952),

Appendix

Columbia (summer, 1964), Univ. of Washington (summer, 1965), Harvard (summer, 1966), Stanford (summer, 1968). Guggenheim fellow (1951–52). Co-editor, *Anglistica*, 1964–. Co-author, *The Effect of Stress upon Vowel Quantity* (1939). Author, *Tarheel Talk: An Historical Study of the English Language in North Carolina to 1860* (1956). Co-editor, *Ælfric's First Series of Catholic Homilies* (1966).

Scope: The complete works of Chaucer.

Description: The main concern of the seminar was Chaucer's literary achievements. The approach was critical rather than linguistic, textual, or biographical. Topics included his language and versification, structural and style, design and meaning; the literary background; and recent trends in Chaucer criticism. Participants were free to concentrate on any of Chaucer's works or any critical problem meriting attention.

II. MONASTICISM IN THE ELEVENTH AND TWELFTH CENTURIES

Senior Fellow: Dr. Giles Constable, H. C. Lea Professor of Medieval History, Harvard University. Assistant editor of *Speculum* (since 1958); member of the Advisory Committee of *The Journal of Ecclesiastical History*, the Executive Committee of the Mediaeval Academy of America, and the Advisory Board of the Institute of Medieval Canon Law. Lecturer, Centre d'Études supérieures de Civilization médiévale at Poitiers (1961). Author and editor: (with James Kritzeck) *Petrus Venerabilis 1156–1956* (Rome, 1956); *Monastic Tithes from their Origins to the Twelfth Century* (1964); *The Letters of Peter the Venerable* (1967).

Scope: Church and spirituality, with some material on other fields (institutions, economic history, art and architecture, liturgy).

Description: The seminar paid particular attention to the development of the new religious orders (Cistercian, Carthusian, Premonstratensian, and other) and their impact on the traditional Benedictine monasticism. The relation of these movements to contemporary social and economic developments was considered.

III. FLORENTINE EARLY RENAISSANCE ART, 1400–1450

Senior Fellow: Dr. H. W. Janson, Professor and Chairman, Fine

Appendix

Arts, Washington Square College, New York University. Visiting
Professor, University of California, Berkeley (1962), Harvard (1967).
Guggenheim Fellow, 1948–49, 1956. Editor, *The Art Bulletin*, 1962–
65; *Sources and Documents, in the History of Art*, 1965–. Author,
Apes and Ape Lore in the Middle Ages and the Renaissance (1952);
The Sculpture of Donatello (1957); *Key Monuments of the History
of Art* (1959); *History of Art* (1962).

Scope: Architecture, sculpture, painting, historiography, intellectual history.

Description: The seminar concentrated on the origins of Early
Renaissance art, on the sources of innovation, on the relation of
artistic theory and practice, and on the evolution of the concept,
"Early Renaissance." A reading knowledge of German, French,
and Italian was required.

IV. THE DYNAMICS OF CULTURAL CHANGE IN THE MEDIEVAL WEST

Senior Fellow: Dr. Lynn White, Jr., Professor of History and Di-
rector of the Center for Medieval and Renaissance Studies, Uni-
versity of California, Los Angeles. Fellow and Vice-president of
Medieval Academy of America; Past President of the Society for
the History of Technology; Vice-president of the History of Science
Society; Fellow of the American Academy of Arts and Sciences;
Member correspondant de l'Académie Internationale d'Histoire
des Sciences; Councillor of the American Historical Association;
Guggenheim Fellow, 1958–59; Winner of the Pfizer Award of the
History of Science Society (1963) and the Leonardo da Vinci Medal
of the Society for the History of Technology (1964); Senior Fellow,
Society for the Humanities, Cornell University, 1968–69; Author,
Latin Monasticism in Norman Sicily (1938, repr. 1968); *Educating
Our Daughters* (1950); ed., *Frontiers of Knowledge* (1956); *Medi-
eval Technology and Social Change* (1962); ed., *The Transforma-
tion of the Roman World* (1966).

Scope: Interdisciplinary: economics, religion, science, technology
and art.

Description: The seminar explored possible applications of some
insights of anthropologists, social psychologists and sociologists into

[159]

Appendix

problems of cultural dynamics in the medieval West. Why did the dynamism of the West differ from that of Byzantium and of Islam? How much cultural change was generated internally, and how much was induced by external influences?

v. Early Renaissance Humanism in Italy (Latin and Italian)

Senior Fellow: Dr. Aldo Scaglione, W. R. Kenan Professor, Romance Languages and Comparative Literature, The University of North Carolina at Chapel Hill. Professor of Italian and Comparative Literature and Chairman of the Italian Department, University of California, Berkeley (1963–65). Visiting Professor, Middlebury Summer School (1953), Yale University (1965). Fulbright Fellow (1951), Guggenheim Fellow (1958), Newberry Library Senior Resident Fellow (1964). Member of the Board of Editors for *Romance Notes, Romance Philology, Studi Francesi*. Editor, M. M. Boiardo, *Orlando Innamorato, Amorum Libri* (1951, 1963, 2 vols.). Author, *Nature and Love in the Late Middle Ages* (1963), *Ars Grammatica* (1968), etc.

Scope: Interdisciplinary: classical philology, cultural history, literary scholarship.

Description: Study of the derivation from Petrarch of the main trends of intellectual and philological endeavors highlighting the evolution of Italian Humanism. Particular emphasis was placed on the role of the new interpretation of the Classics in the transformations which took place within the basic disciplines of linguistic, rhetorical, poetic, philological studies. Exemplary texts were selected for close study and discussion, and the fellows were encouraged to bring forth additional texts on which they were working.

vi. Editorial Problems in Shakespeare

Senior Fellow: Dr. George Walton Williams, Professor of English, Duke University, Durham, N.C. Summer fellowship, Episcopal Theological School, Cambridge, 1958; Summer Fellowship, Folger Shakespeare Library, 1960. Editor of *Renaissance Papers* 1958–. Editor: *Romeo and Juliet* (1964), *The Changeling* (1966), *Henry VI*, Parts 2 and 3 (1967); *Complete Poetry of Richard Crashaw*

(1968); contributing editor, *The Dramatic Works in the Beaumont and Fletcher Canon* (1967–); *More Traditional Ballads of Virginia* (1960). Member editorial board, *Shakespeare Studies* and *Renaissance English Text Society*. Author: *Image and Symbol in the Sacred Poetry of Richard Crashaw* (1963).

Scope: Shakespeare, Elizabethan drama, editing of Elizabethan and Jacobean texts.

Description: The seminar examined the problems of editing printed books of the sixteenth and seventeenth centuries, concentrating on Shakespeare's works. Discussions included some comment on Elizabethan handwriting, analysis of the printing methods of the period, and survey of appropriate techniques in the preparation of modern editions.

Fellows of the Southeastern Institute of Medieval and Renaissance Studies, 1969

SEMINAR NO. 1: Sister Mary Ann Cook (Trinity College)
Bennie Douglas Crenshaw (Middle Tennessee State U.)
James Ivan Miller, Jr. (University of Tulsa)
Jerome Mitchell (University of Georgia)
F. Elaine Penninger (University of Richmond)
Huling E. Ussery, Jr. (Tulane University)

SEMINAR NO. 2: Raymond J. Cormier (University of Virginia)
Alan Darwin Jacobs (Queens College)
Hugh Thomas Keenan (Georgia State College)
Richard William Pfaff (UNC at Chapel Hill)
Katherine Bache Trower (Virginia Polytechnic Institute)

SEMINAR NO. 3: Jerry Draper (Florida State University)
Patricia May Gathercole (Roanoke College)
John Ivan Pav (East Tennessee State University)
Marjorie S. Strauss (Old Dominion College)
Sara Lanier Smythe (UNC at Chapel Hill)
William Henry Trotter (UNC at Chapel Hill)

SEMINAR NO. 4: Sidney Leon Cohen (LSU at Baton Rouge)
Gregory G. Guzman (Bradley University)

Appendix

Douglas J. McMillan (University of Arkansas)
George H. Shriver (Southeastern Baptist
Seminary)
Robert R. Stinson (UNC at Greensboro)
Phillip Drennon Thomas (Wichita State
University)

SEMINAR No. 5: Alvin Larkin Kirkman (Stanford University)
Fleming Greene Vinson (University of Tennessee)
George Burke Johnston (Virginia Polytechnic
Institute)
Alan Richard Perreiah (University of Kentucky)
Cynthia Grant Tucker (Memphis State University)

SEMINAR No. 6: William T. Cocke III (University of the South)
Elmer Richard Gregory, Jr. (University of Toledo)
Robert Hapgood (University of New Hampshire)
Charles Bruce Lower (University of Georgia)
Woodrow Wilson Powell (Georgia Southern
College)
John Racin, Jr. (West Virginia University)